SUICIDAL SOCIOPATH

SURVIVING A SOCIOPATH

BY

KENDIA PERKINS

www.bookstandpublishing.com

Published by
Bookstand Publishing
Morgan Hill, CA 95037
3101_2

Copyright © 2010 by Kendia Perkins
All rights reserved. No part of this publication may be reproduced or transmitted in any form or by any means, electronic or mechanical, including photocopy, recording, or any information storage and retrieval system, without permission in writing from the copyright owner.

ISBN 978-1-58909-1-58909-705-6

Printed in the United States of America

DEDICATION

This book is dedicated to my beautiful Jaja, Yohance, and Omari. You bring me joy everyday of my life. I thank God for you.

Thank you God for your wisdom in this healing process. Thank you God for your Divine protection and guidance.

PROFILE OF THE SOCIOPATH

This profile summarizes some of the common features of descriptions of the behavior of sociopaths.

- Glibness and Superficial Charm
- Manipulative and Conning

They never recognize the rights of others and see their self-serving behaviors as permissible. They appear to be charming, yet are covertly hostile and domineering, seeing their victim as merely an instrument to be used. They may dominate and humiliate their victims.

- Grandiose Sense of Self

Feels entitled to certain things as "their right."

- Pathological Lying

Has no problem lying coolly and easily and it is almost impossible for them to be truthful on a consistent basis. Can create, and get caught up in, a complex belief about their own powers and abilities. Extremely convincing and even able to pass lie detector tests.

- Lack of Remorse, Shame or Guilt

A deep seated rage, which is split off and repressed, is at their core. Does not see others around them as people, but only as targets and opportunities. Instead of friends, they have victims and accomplices who end up as victims. The end always justifies the means and they let nothing stand in their way.

- Shallow Emotions

When they show what seems to be warmth, joy, love and compassion it is more feigned than experienced and serves an ulterior motive. Outraged by insignificant matters, yet remaining unmoved and cold by what would upset a normal person. Since they are not genuine, neither are their promises.

- Incapacity for Love
- Need for Stimulation

Living on the edge. Verbal outbursts and physical punishments are normal. Promiscuity and gambling are common.

- Callousness/Lack of Empathy

Unable to empathize with the pain of their victims, having only contempt for others' feelings of distress and readily taking advantage of them.

- Poor Behavioral Controls/Impulsive Nature

Rage and abuse, alternating with small expressions of love and approval produce an addictive cycle for abuser and abused, as well as creating hopelessness in the victim. Believe they are all-powerful, all-knowing, entitled to every wish, no sense of personal boundaries, no concern for their impact on others.

- Early Behavior Problems/Juvenile Delinquency

Usually has a history of behavioral and academic difficulties, yet "gets by" by conning others. Problems in making and keeping friends; aberrant behaviors such as cruelty to people or animals, stealing, etc.

- Irresponsibility/Unreliability

Not concerned about wrecking others' lives and dreams. Oblivious or indifferent to the devastation they cause. Does not accept blame themselves, but blames others, even for acts they obviously committed.

- Promiscuous Sexual Behavior/Infidelity

Promiscuity, child sexual abuse, rape and sexual acting out of all sorts.

- Lack of Realistic Life Plan/Parasitic Lifestyle

Tends to move around a lot or makes all encompassing promises for the future, poor work ethic but exploits others effectively.

- Criminal or Entrepreneurial Versatility

Changes their image as needed to avoid prosecution. Changes life story readily.

Other Related Qualities:
1. Contemptuous of those who seek to understand them
2. Does not perceive that anything is wrong with them
3. Authoritarian
4. Secretive
5. Paranoid
6. Only rarely in difficulty with the law, but seeks out situations where their tyrannical behavior will be tolerated, condoned, or admired
7. Conventional appearance
8. Goal of enslavement of their victim(s)
9. Exercises despotic control over every aspect of the victim's life
10. Has an emotional need to justify their crimes and therefore needs their victim's affirmation (respect, gratitude and love)
11. Ultimate goal is the creation of a willing victim
12. Incapable of real human attachment to another
13. Unable to feel remorse or guilt
14. Extreme narcissism and grandiose
15. May state readily that their goal is to rule the world

(The above traits are based on the psychopathy checklists of H. Cleckley and R. Hare.)

NOTE: In the 1830's this disorder was called "moral insanity." By 1900 it was changed to "psychopathic personality." More recently it has been termed "antisocial personality disorder" in the DSM-III and DSM-IV. Some critics have complained that, in the attempt to rely only on 'objective' criteria, the DSM has broadened the concept to include too many individuals. The APD category includes people who commit illegal, immoral or self-serving acts for a variety of reasons and are not necessarily psychopaths.

CHAPTER 1

THE MORTGAGE

All of Patrick's dirty business began to surface at one time, November 2007. What was once a happy, trusting home became a battlefield of good versus evil. There was a time when Patrick could do no wrong in Christina's eyes. He was this sweet humble man she had met in undergrad. I mean he was doing it all. Lying, stealing, cheating, smoking, you name it and I guarantee Patrick could claim it. All right up under Christina's nose. Then he slips up majorly, and things would never ever be the same.

Patrick has been crying to Christina everyday from the moment he knew she was thinking of divorcing him. At first he tried to lie his way out of it. The evidence against him was solid. He tries to act like it is no big deal that he has been stealing the mortgage. Christina decides to do some research on a few recent things in the past that had not added up to Patrick's explanations.

The major avalanche for Patrick started when the annual mortgage statement came in the mail. This was a detailed statement regarding monthly payments and rear ages. They were already in bankruptcy because of some previous mishandlings with the mortgage on Patrick's end. In order to keep their home, Christina is paying $850.00 bi-weekly for the next five years. Christina is on a teacher's salary. Patrick is not working at this time.

Christina begins getting the mortgage put in cashier checks. The check is from their credit union with both her and Patrick's name on it. The checks were made out to the bankruptcy trustee. This is to make sure that the mortgage money isn't mishandled again. This way they would not spend it. The mortgage statement arrives by mail. Christina immediately notices that there are five months of payments missing. She doesn't panic because she has kept all of the cashier check receipts.

The two of them go to see their bankruptcy attorney to discuss the issue. The attorney explains that she needs the official statements from the credit union in order to correct the situation. The attorney goes on to explain that she had seen in the past that when one spouse thinks the other is paying the mortgage actually they are doing something else with the money. This is the reason that the proof has to come from the credit union. Needless to say a light bulb went off in Christina's head.

Afterwards, in the attorney's parking lot, Christina asked Patrick "have you been taking the mortgage money?" Patrick says "NO!" Christina reiterates were you spending the money on that Nina woman? "No, I swear to God I wasn't giving her a dime! I have no more lies or secrets. I've learned my lesson." Christina takes a breather; "Ok Patrick, we will let the bank figure out the error."

Christina continues research into the matter. This is 5 months of mortgage, hard earned money. Patrick sits there as if he has nothing to do with it. He acts as if it's the credit union's fault again. The previous mortgage incidence was blamed on the mortgage company. Christina didn't have any receipts that time. She couldn't prove anything. But this time around is totally different. She has all of her receipts-every last one of them.

Christina finds that the mortgage checks have been resubmitted to the bank for pay out. She is livid. She asked the bank teller who could do this? The teller says only 3 parties-you, your husband or the trustee. The teller goes on to say that the checks in question were not cashed by the trustee. This leads to only one conclusion-Patrick. Christina knows that she hadn't cashed any.

Christina confronts Patrick again. Patrick has the nerve to tell her that she told him to cash the checks. He tells her that she was moving some money around. Christina tells him that he is a mother fucking liar. It is amazing that Patrick has the nerve to act like she is crazy. He can be so convincing that if you are not on your p's and q's you would begin to question yourself. However, this didn't work with Christina. After all, she is the person he is trying to blame. Finally, the teller calls back with the proof that every one of the resubmitted mortgage checks were resubmitted and cashed by Patrick. They have his signatures.

Now, Patrick realizes that the cat is out of the bag. He goes into confession mold. "Ok, yes I took some money. I just wanted to do what I wanted to do." Christina begins to cry. She says, "That's it, I am divorcing you." "You're going to divorce me because I took a little money." Patrick has a way of minimizing everything that he does. "No, I'm divorcing you because you stole the mortgage for 5 months. This is me and my children's livihood." He pretends that Christina is overreacting.

The one thing that Patrick knows about Christina is that she doesn't stay angry for long. He knows that Christina values family over any sort of material possession. Basically, he hopes that time would make this better. He only wants to weather this storm. He thinks that Christina would somehow take some kind of responsibility for her part. This would be giving him a way out without taking full responsibility for his actions.

Patrick has underestimated Christina. Christina reflects and becomes angrier. This is what she replays in her mind. She is pregnant at the time Patrick is stealing the mortgage. She would give Patrick the cashier checks to mail the mortgage. This scandalous ass man would take that check to the bank and cash it for himself! Then, he would bring her the receipts as if he mailed the checks. He did this 10 times. He started stealing the money in December 2007 and continued through April 2008. The last check he stole was while she was in the hospital after having a c-section with their last son. The reason he stopped is because Christina went back to handling the household finances. The manipulation and calculation is more bothersome than anything else.

The more she thinks about the situation, the more she sees red. She had resigned from her job and pulled down her early retirement to cover being off work for maternity leave. The plan was that Patrick would get a job teaching and be the bread winner for awhile. She remembers being in the hospital trying to decide how to pay for a rental car to get from the hospital to home with the new beautiful baby boy. She even went into the negative with the credit union to cover the expenses until her maternity insurance paid out. All the while Patrick was stealing the mortgage.

Christina wants to know what Patrick has done with all of this money. She hadn't noticed anything different. She asked him if he is on drugs? He says no. She knows there is nothing that he can tell her that would make her understand why he would steal from her and the children, especially while she was pregnant.

Now is the time when a girl needs good counsel. She needs someone with a clear head that has her best interest at heart. This is Christina's best friend Samone. Samone's question to Christina is what do you do now? You have to make a plan. Samone explained to Christina that she has to take the focus off of Patrick right now. She has to do what is best for her and the children. This proves to be the best advice Christina received during this time.

CHAPTER 2

SEARCHING FOR ANSWERS REGARDING STOLEN MORTGAGE—WOMAN'S APARTMENT

While Patrick was wondering about being manipulative with his crying and promising to be a better person, Christina decides to research to find out exactly what the hell Patrick did with all that money. She begins with locating his previous found infidelity. She wants to know if Patrick got her pregnant and was giving her their mortgage money. Sure enough Christina finds the woman. Wouldn't you know it, she lives right around the corner from their home-one mile away. The internet is a wonderful tool.

At this point Christina needs answers; clearly Patrick refuses to be honest about anything. She feels desperate. Against Samone's advice Christina goes to the woman's apartment. The woman answers the door. The woman knows who Christina is because she has seen her before. However, Christina doesn't know what she looks like. The woman asked Christina why is she here. Christina says that she has some questions that she would like to ask her regarding her involvement with Patrick her husband. The woman responds with "why should I tell you anything? That was months ago and I have moved on. I have a new man and have not talked to Patrick since all of that happened." She tells Christina that she doesn't owe her anything. She goes on to say that if she can give her one good reason why she should talk to her then she would consider it. Christina simply says that she is desperate. She needs answers about the man that she has lived with as her husband for the past 8 years. There has been mortgage money missing. She told her that she wants to know if she had a baby by Patrick or if he was giving her money when they dated.

The woman lets down her guard and obliges. She says no she did not get pregnant by Patrick. They used protection. She explains that she is a single mother with two children and in college. She says that she was not trying to have any more children. Christina asked a series of questions from there.

Christina: Why did you protect Patrick when we called you by saying that you weren't sleeping with him?

Woman: I thought that he was a nice and cool dude. Patrick told me that you were his crazy ex wife trying to take his one son away from him and take him for all the money he has. Patrick told me that he needed me to tell you that nothing happened because you were crazy. He kept calling me telling me to say this and that. Finally, I told him that this is elementary and he should have told me that he was married.

Christina: How did you two meet?

Woman: We met at the bowling alley.

Christina: Did he come on to you or vice versa?

Patrick told me that you sucked his dick in the bowling alley parking lot and allowed him to cum in your mouth. That is what he told me the fascination was with you.

Woman: I hate when men tell the story to make them look good. He is a lie. Even if that were true, he was cheating. It doesn't matter how he was cheating.

Patrick asked for my number at the bowling alley. He said that he could fix my moms computer. He called to get directions to my mom's house. After he was done he called me and honestly I thought that he was calling to say he had completed the job. Instead, he said that he was trying to get with me and wanted to know when he could take me out. We went out the next night after bowling at this place on Main and Livingston. He paid for my meal that time but that was the only thing he had paid on my behalf. We started fucking from then.

Our affair lasted for about 3-4 months. He would bring me over burned DVD movies because he knew that I liked movies. I thought he might have had a girlfriend but never a wife. He would come over at about 1am and leave shortly afterwards saying he had deliveries. He would never kiss me in the mouth.

Patrick invited me and my girlfriend on a double date with one of his cousins that came to town from the south. Patrick told us to order what we wanted and then the cousin came in and told the server to put our orders on his tab; Patrick didn't even pay for that.

I liked Patrick because he was a mysterious, cool dude and a good fuck. I didn't know anything about a wife until I called and you answered his phone.

Christina: Wow, the note that you left by the waitress was a classic. Why did you leave it after protecting him previously? Why didn't you come over to the table yourself?

Woman: That was a classic huh, they both laugh, but I left the note to let you know that I knew Patrick more than he had told you. The nerve of him to walk into that restaurant with you and look at me as if he had never seen me in his life. Yes, I wanted to fuck his night up.

Christina: Girl, the crazy thing is that mother fucker didn't even act nervous. I wouldn't have known that you were there-thanks for the note. Then, he tried to say that you were crazy and trying to start some shit between us because he told you that he could no longer be associated with you. Remember, in his story you two weren't fucking. And, he used you to convince me of that.

Woman: Again, I am sorry. I did not know that he was married. I was pissed off that he didn't give me the opportunity to make a choice. The truth is that if I like you I will sleep with you married or not. Patrick didn't give me the choice.

Christina: Thank you so much, I will not bother you ever again. I appreciate your honesty.

WOMAN: Ok

CHAPTER 3

WHAT LED CHRISTINA TO THE WOMANS HOUSE — NINA?

Well, by now this woman deserves a name; her name is Nina. Nina came on the scene in July, as a matter of fact July 13, 2007, Christina's birthday. It was the night before her big day. Patrick, Christina and the kids are on a road trip to visit Christina's family in Chicago. They have just arrived into the city. They need to get her brothers new address. Christina doesn't remember how to get to the new house. She needs to call him. Patrick passes his cell phone to Christina. She is sitting in the back seat. Christina calls her brother and gets the directions. The brief moment that Christina has Patrick's phone a text message comes through. It reads-"I want to see you tonight, can you come over to my place? Let me know one way or the other-Nina"

Now, Christina has always put her cards on the table too soon. This has always led to Patrick being several steps ahead of her. The children are in the car. Christina keeps her composure for the moment. At least until they get to her brothers new home. The only thing she says while in the car is "oooh, somebody has been living foul." Patrick immediately gets nervous and starts stuttering but at the same time trying to keep his cool. Patrick says "help me look for your brother's place." Christina responds to the text with "Yes, I can come over for an after party to get busy." Christina wants to see Nina's response. When she ask Patrick who is Nina she can some proof.

However, Nina doesn't respond. Christina tells Patrick that she is going to hold on to his cell phone until the morning. Christina ask Patrick who the hell is Nina? Of course, this fool says he doesn't know anyone by that name. Why is she texting you about coming over? Patrick says he doesn't know. "Ok, Mr. Fucking I Don't Know." She goes to bed furious that Nina has not responded and that Patrick is lying. She knows he would try contacting Nina to cover his ass before she contacts her. Christina sleeps with the cell phone in her purse next to her bed. She thinks that Patrick only has her number programmed in his phone. She hopes that he doesn't know it by heart.

Christina wakes up with butterflies on her stomach. It's her birthday and the only got damn gift Patrick has for her is an affair! Nina sends Patrick a text message. It reads that she didn't get his messages until late but she hopes that everything is ok with him.

Christina can be somewhat naïve, that's where Samone comes in. Samone explains to Christina that Patrick had been trying to call Nina to cover his ass. She tells her that the text response from Nina doesn't coincide with the text that she had sent her about after party and getting busy.

Nina calls Patrick early that morning. Christina answers hello. Nina says "who is this answering his phone?" She acts like she is Patrick's woman and is ready to kick some ass. "Calm down, I am Patrick's sister; he's asleep and asked me to answer his phone." Nina becomes all friendly and says "oh, hey and how are you?" So Christina says "I'm fine who is this and how do you know my little brother?" "I'm Nina and we bowl together, I mean not together but in the same league."

Now, Christina knows for sure that Patrick is lying about not knowing any Nina. "What is your relationship with my brother?" Nina gets suspicious and defensive." Have Patrick call me!" She immediately hangs up the phone.

Christina loses her mind! She and Patrick go out in her brother's back yard. At this moment, her family has no idea of anything going on. Christina has a birthday cook out planned. She has invited all of her family members. She is trying to keep Patrick from screwing up her entire birthday. She is a huge birthday person and believes in celebrating to the fullest.

This birthday isn't quite turning out that way. She starts to yell at Patrick about having an affair on her with this Nina. She tells him that he can stop lying because she spoke with the woman. In her rage she throws his cell phone to the ground and bust that shit up. Patrick picks his phone up and attempts to put it back together again.

He tries to explain to Christina that those are chain emails sent from different people. His story is that he met some people at the bowling alley through Christina's co-worker Andrew. He says that Andrew gave his number out saying that he could do almost any home improvements. That's how Nina got his number but he doesn't know her personally. She always send him flirtatious texts but that's all to it. By this time, Christina's brother knows that something is wrong. Christina knows that Patrick is lying and tries anyway to go through with her birthday celebration.

Christina calls Nina back from her own cell phone this time. She tells Nina that Patrick is her husband. She wants to know the nature of their relationship. Nina says, "Ask your man, bitch." Christina, keeping her cool with Nina letting her know that she does not have an issue with her. She continues to ask Nina the same question-what is your relationship with Patrick? Nina finally says he's my movie guy-I buy burned movies from him, now are you satisfied?

Christina says not quite, if he's your movie man why did you text him stating that you wanted to see him can he come over? Nina says that wasn't exactly what she texted. Why are you asking me why don't you question your man or is he your brother? Christina explains to her that the reason she called her is because Patrick is denying even knowing her. She hopes that she could get some answers from her. "Where does he sell you movies?" Nina says all over, the bowling alley, he brings them to my apartment. This just gives Christina more evidence that Patrick is still lying about knowing Nina. This means that there is something huge to hide. They both hang up the phone.

She goes to Patrick and says let's call Nina. I will be on one cordless and you on the other. Patrick agrees, thinking that he's already talked to his alibi so, why not. Christina places the call

11

but Patrick could not speak or hear on the other cordless. However, right after the call Patrick's cell phone rings.

Christina knows it is Nina calling Patrick back. She can't prove it because she had already busted up the damn phone. She can't even go through and check the text message that started everything or previous messaging. Christina later realizes that you can't use two cordless phones at the same time.

By now the kids are awake. They are singing happy birthday to Christina. The nerve of Patrick to be joining in like everything is all good. That makes Christina sick to her stomach, just the thought of him. Patrick goes for a walk. He basically goes to put his alibi and plan together to get Christina off his case. This is when he decides to call in Andrew, a known womanizer, Christina's co-worker. Patrick met Andrew through Christina. Christina and Andrew taught and coached at the same school. Patrick figured if he could get Andrew to collaborate his story then he would be in the clear. He figures that Christina would never suspect Andrew to lie to her.

Closer and closer to the barbecue Christina just can't keep it together. She decides that the whole thing is off. She is going to leave Patrick's cheating ass right there in Chicago and let him have Nina pick his ass up.

She packs the children up in the van and loads the luggage. The entire time, the children and their cousins are crying because they don't know what has happened. Christina's sister in law, Stephanie, doesn't know what to do. She calls Christina's aunt. Her brother isn't there to at least stop her. He would talk some sense into her about driving all that way at night with the children. Christina gets on the road then about 20 minutes away the new born baby starts crying and wouldn't stop. That brings Christina back to her senses. She quickly turns around and goes back to her brother's home.

By this time the entire family is there. However, they don't have a clue as to what is going on. All they know is that she had hit the road leaving her husband behind. She wasn't quite ready to talk about the situation with anyone. Right after the barbeque Christina, Patrick, and the children get back on the road for home.

Patrick drives the entire way. Patrick had pitched the co-worker story to Christina's brother. Wesley speaks with her. He tells her that he believes Patrick. He doesn't think that Patrick is cheating on her.

On the trip back Patrick tells Christina the story again. He tells her the reason he said that he didn't know Nina is because he didn't know how to explain her without looking guilty of having an affair. Christina still doesn't believe Patrick but she is glad that he is driving the family back Ohio.

The next day, Christina tells Patrick to call Nina from their home phone and just talk to her. He says why because he doesn't know her like that. He agrees and calls Nina. Nina talks to Patrick as if she has known him forever and a day.

All hell breaks loose after that. She tells Patrick again that he is lying about the details of their relationship. Patrick gets violent. He starts swearing and throwing tables around the room. He's home now so he figures if he acts a damn fool then maybe Christina will leave this alone. He would never have acted like that around Christina's family. He scares Christina. Samone tells her to lay off the situation. Christina refuses because she hasn't done anything wrong.

Patrick leaves the house going for a walk. You know the walks he has to take to get his story straight. He calls Nina. He tells her what he needs her to say. Nina agrees because he has informed her that Christina is his crazy ex wife.

He tells her that if she finds out that they were together she would be able to take his son and all of his money. First of all, Patrick has three children not just one. Second of all, Patrick doesn't have any money. Patrick is as broke as he is unemployed.

When Patrick gets back to the house he apologizes for his behavior. He says lets call her back. Christina agrees. What Patrick doesn't anticipate is that Christina would have a list of questions for him to ask Nina. So, whatever he has rehearsed with Nina was a mute point because the questions were different. They call and he proceeds to ask Nina questions which she was not responding well because she didn't have the answers.

Afterwards, Patrick says to Christina "see I told you there is nothing between us." Christina says what conversation were you listening to? Patrick just wants Christina to leave it alone.

Late that night Christina has Patrick call Nina back. He says to her that he has jeopardized his marriage and family by associating with her. He tells her that he loves his family and he needs her to lose his number. No more texting him. Nina responds with "y'all still thinking about me? Ok fine, this is ridiculous because nothing happened between us!"

CHAPTER 4

SUICIDE THREAT

Christina doesn't believe Patrick or Nina for one second. Patrick insists that Christina is blaming him for something that was not true. Patrick is desperate. He goes into the basement and gets the shot gun. He tells her that he will kill himself if he lost his family over a lie. He walks through the house saying that he doesn't want to be a statistic. He's saying aloud to himself, "that's a bad idea man. Don't do that to your family." By now, Christina is terrified of Patrick. All of the sudden, he puts the shot gun in the closet. He leaves the house. Christina calls her sister Rita. She tells her what just happened. She calls Samone. Samone told her that she is scared for her. She begs Christina to let it go. Christina agrees.

Later, Rita calls Christina back telling her that Patrick is at her house. Christina tells Rita to ask Patrick to please come home. She says that they can work things out. Patrick is there for about an hour. He tells Rita that he doesn't know Nina. He says that he has never cheated on Christina. He says that he is going to blow his brains out if Christina believes Nina over him. He will not live without his family. Rita tells Patrick that he needs to be honest. She says that nothing is worth taking your own life. Patrick ask Rita if she can talk to her sister. Rita says yes she will talk to her but he needs to go home. Patrick departs and goes home.

Rita calls Christina right after Patrick departs. She tells her of their conversation. She advises her to let it go. She tells her that Patrick is lying but to let it go anyway. She says that Patrick is in bad shape. She doesn't trust his mental stability. "Call me when he gets there."

Patrick arrives home. He says that he loves his family. He begins crying like a little boy. Christina gets really nervous. She doesn't know his mindset. She doesn't want to become the evening news. She eases up. She tells him that nothing is that serious. She says that they would be devastated if he committed suicide. They begin to communicate.

Patrick expresses to Christina that all his life he has been blamed for things that he did not do. Christina sits and listens attentively. Patrick says that when he was a kid people would do bad things. He would tell them to say that he did it. He was blamed for everything any way. He swears that is the story of his life. She ask him if he thought that he was in the wrong in this situation. He looks at her wiping his tears and says "I don't know that woman". She feels sorry for him because he is crying. However, she knows that there is a lot more to this story.

Samone tells her to let it go. It is not that important any more. Christina chooses to let it go and move forward. Truth is she hadn't planned on divorcing Patrick over an affair. She would simply sleep with whomever she wants from this point on and that would be getting him back enough. At this point Christina decided that she would no longer be this faithful friend and wife to Patrick. She feels that Patrick has got away with something major. It's not fair that he played the suicide card.

Christina takes a little trip to Atlanta. She has a little sexual rendezvous with an old friend. She doesn't quite get the satisfaction that she is searching. This did the job in helping her move forward. Patrick picks her up from the airport. She looks at him with disgust. He is acting as if he is so happy to see her. She feels like their marriage is now one big lie.

She and Patrick decide that they would work on their marriage. However, Christina doesn't feel that she needs to do anything more. She is paying all the bills, being respectful to Patrick, and fucking him whenever he wants. It is tough for her but she didn't get the answers she needed to make a more informed decision; She does what many other women do, she presses forward with the liar and cheater. Christina doesn't know what more she can give without losing herself.

CHAPTER 5

ANDREW THE ALIBI

Several weeks after they decide to work on their marriage, Nina reenters the scene. Patrick and Christina are at a seafood restaurant after an evening of golf. They are in the restaurant talking and eating dinner. At about the end of their meal a waitress comes over. The waitress brings a Corona with lime and a note for Patrick. The note reads "enjoy and I hope to see you soon." It has a big smiley face on it. The waitress feels really bad because she feels that she has started a conflict. Christina explains to her that she has not. She thanks her for bringing it over. She asked the server "where is this person." She tells her that she had left already.

Nina asked that she not give them the note and beer until she was gone. Christina ask a few questions about the appearance of the woman and if she paid with a credit card. That was the missing piece to the puzzle. Yes, she had paid with a credit card. The waitress tells her Nina's last name. That is how Christina was able to track Nina down when she needed answers regarding the stolen mortgage.

This experience has Christina so paranoid. Everywhere she goes she wonders if she sees a woman fitting the description that the waitress had given of Nina. This takes Patrick and Christina back to square 1. It is as if they never got anywhere. Patrick tries to pretend that Nina is some chick that is trying to cause trouble for them. He decides to use his trump card. He says lets call Andrew. He will tell you that this chick is crazy. Christina says ok, lets call Andrew.

They call Andrew. Andrew has been avoiding Christina's calls since this entire fiasco began. Andrew and Christina are pretty good friends. Patrick has underestimated their friendship. Patrick calls Andrew from his cell phone. Andrew answers and Patrick tells him that his wife wants to talk to him. Christina gets on the phone; she goes into a series of questions for Andrew. He starts lying for Patrick. Andrew tells Christina that he has been involved with Nina. However, he can't tell her Nina's last name. He didn't know where she lived. He basically gets defensive and says "look Christina, I do not want to be badgered on trial. I'm not answering anymore of your questions. I am about hang up the phone."

Christina can't believe Andrew had behaved like that with her. Andrew acted like she was upset with him. The truth is Andrew was upset with Patrick. He did not want to be brought into that situation.

Christina goes to her former school; the first person she sees is Andrew. They both look at each other then hug. The first words out of Christina's mouth are "man, what the hell was that?" Another bomb shell drops. Andrew tells Christina that Patrick called him recently. He says "if Christina calls you and ask you about a woman named Nina, I need you to tell her that you are dating her." Andrew says that he agreed because of some male code. Andrew says that he has covered for other male friends in the past; however, none of those women were his friend.

Andrew apologizes for treating Christina in such a way. He explains to her that he just loves her family. He thinks that she and Patrick are the perfect married couple. He didn't want to see something Patrick does as a man destroy that.

He goes on to say that he doesn't even know this woman. He confesses how bad he felt for lying to her. Christina is in shock. "You don't know the woman?" Andrew says no, I haven't been to any bowling alley with Patrick. The story he has given you is completely false.

Christina confronts Patrick with what Andrew has told her. Patrick has the nerve to say that Andrew is lying to her. He wants to know why she is still asking questions regarding Nina. He tells her that he thought they were over that. He doesn't know why Andrew is lying to her. He says that Andrew wants her for himself. She completely ignores his logic. He was trying to divert the conversation.

Christina gives Patrick an ultimatum. She tells him that either he gives her more answers or she will be forced to file for divorce. She completely doesn't trust him. She also explains to him that he and Nina are on the same team. They are protecting each other. He sat in that restaurant the entire time knowing that Nina was there. He did not appear to be nervous or anything. Christina starts to feel that Patrick is capable of anything.

Patrick decides to write Christina a letter supposedly detailing the relationship between him and Nina. Patrick says that he met her at the bowling alley. They went to the car to smoke some marijuana. She asked him if she could suck his dick. Patrick said that Nina sucked his dick and let him cum in her mouth. He swore that he did not screw her. He says that she had been trying to get him to come over to her house so they could fuck. He would keep stringing her along. But every bowling night he would go to the car, smoke and get his dick sucked. Christina just didn't buy the fact that a woman would suck a dick in the car, let a man cum in her mouth and not fuck him.

Patrick claims that he had his hands in her pants but that was the extent of it. He claimed that he didn't want to fuck her because he had already cum in her mouth. Christina feels a little relieved that Patrick had come clean about something other than he didn't know the woman.

In this weird way that was actually a turn on. What the hell? Christina is turned on by the thought of some other woman sucking her husband's dick. Patrick explains to Christina that there were no feelings with Nina just sex. He said that because she had a C-section they couldn't have sex.

He basically put some of the responsibility onto Christina. She accepts that. She began to doubt herself. She began to ask him why he felt the need to cheat on her. She can't figure that one out. Christina feels that she takes good care of her man.

Wow, can you believe he gets out of his deceit by using reverse psychology. He tells Christina that he would like to fuck more. He wants to be more inventive with the ways they did it. He doesn't want to always do it in the bed. Can you believe this guy, he starts making requests.

Christina asked him more experimental how? What do you mean you want to fuck more? You're sleep after one session. Christina tells Patrick that she isn't letting anyone cum in her mouth. He says that isn't what he wants from her.

They move on from there. Time passes Christina doesn't trust Patrick not one bit. However, she understands the need to want sex from a different person. After all, Patrick isn't rocking her world, but he has enough bang to keep her content. She expresses to Patrick that she has desires to venture into sex with another man. She didn't have anyone in particular in mind. She feels if he was able to enjoy that gratification then why she shouldn't be able.

Patrick is a bit uncomfortable with this but he knows protesting this would only lead back to his infidelity. He basically listens without much comment. The only thing he does tell Christina is that he wants to be the only man that she is fucking. It makes him feel insecure to think of her and someone else.

However, Patrick knows that Christina isn't the type to play the field, she is the family type. He just wants this phase over. Time passes and things get easier. Christina doesn't hold on to things for very long. She feels that it is too stressful.

CHAPTER 6

RETURN OF THE TRUCK: THE SEARCH FOR ANSWERS REGARDING THE STOLEN MORTGAGE

Christina goes to meet with Andrew. She explains to him how the mortgage money is missing. "Patrick buys weed from me, that's about the extent of our relationship." She asked if Patrick had ever purchased anything other than marijuana from him. Andrew says "no, only Dro -which is like the strongest weed. It is also the more expensive." Andrew explains to Christina that Patrick had mentioned to him before that he was gambling with some guys at the bowling alley. Andrew tells Christina that he is a recovering gambler and he thinks Patrick was gambling that money away.

He explains that after gamblers lose the money, they're upset initially. You think that you can win it back and you keep gambling until you lose everything. He explains that based on the patterns of Patrick taking the money that's what it sounds like to him. Then more dirt comes out.

Andrew calls his father. His father tells him that Patrick owes him $900 for a pick up truck that they had purchased from him. Patrick was supposedly working some overnight deliveries with the truck. Come to find out, the only over night deliveries Patrick were doing were sperm deposits into Nina. That didn't pay anything at least not to Christina. Christina was blown away because she had been giving Patrick $150 per month to pay Dr. Taylor. Patrick would come home telling Christina that Dr. Taylor said hi.

"OMG! What else is this guy covering up? Who is this man that I have been married to for the last 8 years?" Andrew explains to Christina that this is only a molecule of what Patrick has been doing. He expresses his sadness that she is experiencing this drama. However, Andrew tells Christina that his dad Dr. Taylor had been telling him that there was something not quite honest about Patrick. Andrew would always say to his dad "no, he's good people."

Christina makes arrangements with Andrew and his dad to return the truck. Christina apologizes continuously. Christina gives Dr. Taylor a call. She discussed the matter in detail with him. Christina ask Dr. Taylor how can a person do all of this to his family. Dr. Taylor simply says that he has no conscious. He explains that he has been in behavioral science for nearly 30 years. He has seen all types of people. He goes on to explain that Patrick has been lying since he was a kid, probably to cover up some type of misfortune he experienced.

These type of people create fantasy worlds, usually as defense mechanisms. When they become adults they continue with this same pattern of lies. It eventually cost them everything. Instead of feeling remorse for the pain that they have caused others, they continue to convince themselves that they did nothing wrong. They portray themselves as the victim. The sad truth of it all is that they move on to the next victims. Patrick is a SOCIOPATH.

"Patrick has grown up around men that have been liars, cheaters, thieves, and you name it. That is what Patrick knows. When people like that get caught they cry." He wants her to remember that the crying is not because they hurt you but because they have been caught. He tells her that she should do what she needs to in order to protect herself and children. These types of people continue doing all of the same things just to different people until they are caught.

"These types of people never take responsibility for their actions. They always blame other people. They say other people caused them to mistreat them. This is a very dangerous cycle. Confronting a SOCIOPATH liar can become dangerous to both you and the kids. It is best removing yourself from this situation."

Christina explains to Patrick that she has spoken to Dr. Taylor. She told Dr.Taylor that she had given him the money for the truck. She told Dr. Taylor that Patrick had been returning home saying that he said hello and thanks for the payment. Patrick's only question to Christina is why did you talk to him about what's going on with us? Christina is baffled. Are you crazy? I spoke with him because we have his truck. You have not paid him. You have been saying that you had. She tells him that she needs to clear her name.

The crazy thing about this situation is that Patrick only used the truck for about one month. Afterwards, he said that it was using too much gas. They had already made an agreement so they put the truck up for sell. The goal was to pay Dr. Taylor off and possibly make a little profit.

Patrick had taken the truck to his new work site at the airport. The day they were to return the truck Christina wasn't even sure if Patrick still had the truck. She thought that he was lying again. They arrive at the airport parking lot. Patrick did still have the truck. Christina gave a sigh of relief.

They take the truck to Dr. Taylor. Patrick was acting like nothing had happened. He was acting as if they had rented this mans truck and returned it as contracted. Patrick is shaking hands and telling Dr. Taylor that they should go hunting and fishing soon. Christina is amazed. She was thinking what the hell is he doing? She can't believe that he was acting like that. She was so apologetic and ashamed.

Dr. Taylor had told her in their earlier conversation that he would not mention anything to Patrick. But he suggested to Christina that she should get as far away from Patrick as necessary. He explained that he can put her and the kids in a worse situation. Dr. Taylor tells her that Patrick is a con artist and only cares about his own well being.

CHAPTER 7

THE DECISION TO CO EXIST

After all of this new found discovery, Christina asked Patrick to leave their home. She asked him for his key. He gives it to her. Patrick leaves that night in a snowing blizzard. Patrick isn't gone an hour before calling Christina back asking her to come home. He claims that he has no where to go. She tells him to go over to Nina's house or to hell. Either way, it didn't matter much to her.

Patrick called saying that he wants to be able to see his children. She tells him he should have thought of them when he was stealing the roof from over their heads. This went on for about 3 days or so.

While Patrick is out Christina explains to the children that she will be divorcing Patrick. They cry and cry. She holds them. She explains to them that they aren't getting a divorce from their dad. She tells them that they will have two families instead of one. It didn't matter what she said, they knew that divorce isn't good. They don't want their family to be split. She holds them. She tells them that she is so sorry they have to experience this. Afterwards, she tells Patrick that she told the children they are divorcing. She needs to make it clear to him that they are over. Patrick knew that she was serious if she told the kids.

Patrick consults with his sisters. Afterwards, he decides that Christina can't put him out. He tells Christina that it is his house. They will just have to co exist. Christina is so angry. She tells him that if he doesn't leave then she and the children would. He tells her that she isn't taking the children anywhere. Christina begins to pack things for her and the children. Patrick hits her in her head with his fist. He takes away the children's things. She quickly calls the police.

The police come. They can't believe that the call is for a domestic situation. When they arrive everything seems to be calm. Christina doesn't want her children to witness anything violent; Therefore, the situation has calmed down. Christina explains what happened and asked if they can make him leave. Patrick is so calm. It appears that Christina is crazy. The police tell Christina that they can't make Patrick give up the keys to his house. As a matter of fact, they state that they wouldn't give up their keys. Patrick is chuckling with the male officers as if they are buddies. They suggest that Patrick leave the premises for the night. Patrick agreed. Christina couldn't believe that the officers were behaving this way. She understands why so many women are battered and feel that they don't have anywhere to turn.

By this time Patrick is getting counsel from his sisters. They don't like Christina. They feel that Christina was the controller in the marriage. They tell Patrick that he shouldn't allow her any more control. Patrick tells Christina that he doesn't care if she hates his guts but he is not leaving.

Patrick tells Christina that he is angry with her for calling the police on him. He says that she put him out in the blizzard and that he was sleeping in his car. He feels that gives him the right to act any way he wants towards her. Patrick has totally placed blame on Christina for their current situation.

Christina realizes that she must deal with Patrick delicately to maintain her and the children's safety. Christina has some major decisions to make. She needs to weigh the pros and cons of their marriage. She needs some time away out side of the situation.

Christina is hurt, angry and horny. What a combination. She thinks even if she did fuck Patrick it wouldn't change the situation. However, Samone disagree. Samone tells Christina that if she has sex with Patrick he would begin to think that she is getting over things. She was right. In his mind, Christina would be forgiving him. Christina can't let Patrick think that he is off the hook. If she does have sex with him then she would be right back to square one. The violence would probably escalate.

She decides to fly down to Orlando. She gets her sexual needs met by her college sweetheart. She and Lou have always kept in contact with one another. Lou has been separated from his wife for a few months. He is living with his sister until he could afford to get his own place. Even though Lou isn't living home with his family, he is paying the mortgage.

She explains to him what she is going through. She tells him that she needed some sex and it couldn't be with Patrick. He tells her to come on down. He says let him know when and where to meet her. She says "I'll be there when you get off work this evening." He says, "You know I'll take care of you. I can't wait to see you." He becomes her go to guy for sex during this time. This was the power that Christina needed to make better decisions regarding her marriage/divorce.

CHAPTER 8

THE AGONY OF FINDING OUT

Patrick pleads with Christina to not let 20 years go down the drain. He tells her he knows that he messed up. He wants the chance to prove to her that he is a good person. He cries everyday. She wants to know what he did with all the money he had stolen. She begins to ask him a series of questions. "Why did you do this to us? How could you fuck over me and my children?" She tells him that she has treated him better than his parents ever treated him. Christina just can't understand. She is so hurt. She wants Patrick to tell her something that makes sense.

Patrick has nothing but more lies. He says that he was gambling. She doesn't believe that. She continues to ask him if he is on drugs like his brothers, cousins and uncles. He denies that. She is so upset with herself for not having a clue. She isn't around people that use drugs so she wouldn't know what the signs were. Unless it is the classic stereo type of a drug addict on television, she would not know. However, for a person to steal the mortgage while his wife is in the hospital recovering from a C-section is clue enough. Patrick is on something, she just don't know what.

Christina talks with her sisters. The two of them are a bit more street savvy than her. They had both been around people that have sold and used drugs. Rita says that it sounds like a crack head. Crystal thinks that Patrick is too calm with his children for it to be crack. She thinks it might be cocaine.

Christina describes that Patrick would be looking wide and glassy eyed sometimes. She says that he came to the hospital late at night and said that the car caught a flat. At the time, she thinks nothing of it. He was actually looking glassy eyed then. This was the last time he had stolen the mortgage.

Christina tells Patrick that wife privileges are over. When she cooks it is for the kids only. She tells him that he will be nothing without her. She says that she hopes he ends up like the rest of the men in his family. She is so angry with him that she can spit in his face. She feels that neither she nor the children deserved this treatment from Patrick. She wants him to suffer and pay for what he has done to them. She tells him that this would be a really good time to kill himself. She doesn't mean it. However, she's angry and feels he deserves it.

When Christina is alone in her bedroom, she cries. She just can't believe that the one person that promised to care for her would betray her in such a way. She doesn't know how to move through this. If he would jeopardize her and the kid's livelihood, why would she care about him? Christina wants to know what she had done to Patrick to deserve the betrayal.

Patrick tells her in an earlier conversation that the reason he took the money from her is because he had access to it. He told her that he had the affair because he hadn't had sex since the baby. She blames herself for not seeing all of this before now.

CHAPTER 9

PERSPECTIVE — REFOCUSING ENERGY

Christina reconnects with an old friend, Damon. They met in Orlando after undergrad. They dated very briefly and decided they were better as platonic friends. She hadn't spoken with Damon in nine years. When she relocated from Orlando, they lost communication. She located him by doing a Google search online. She got his phone number from there. When she called Damon, he was very happy to hear from her. He had told her that he had been looking for her. He knew she had written a book.

He said that he wanted to see her. She made arrangements to fly down for a weekend. After all, she needed the break. She wanted to go some where and be with someone safe.

The day of her flight, she couldn't fly standby. She called Damon and explained to him the situation. He said "no problem, here is my credit card number. I want you to call and get a flight here to New Orleans tonight." Christina was so use to paying for everything in her relationship with Patrick; She had forgot that there are independent, working men in the world. She felt really special that after years of no communication that Damon would still trust and look out for her.

She flew to New Orleans that night. They went to dinner and the casino the first night she was there. He took care of everything. He even gave her money to gamble. They had such a good time. They caught up on the missing years. She thanked him for the breath of fresh air. Damon was going through some soul searching of his own. He had just got out of a five year engagement. They both shared their current situations. They offered each other advice from male and female perspectives.

When they finally made it to Damon's home, they were both exhausted. He gave her his bedroom and he slept in the guest room. He was such the gentleman. He explained to Christina that she deserved to be treated nothing less than what she experienced with him. He said that she was beautiful and that Patrick is a fool.

Christina felt the wonderful thing about Damon is that he didn't even try to have sex with her. It was such a perfect trip. The next day, they slept in and had breakfast at the house. Later on that afternoon, Damon took her around New Orleans for some sight seeing. He took her to a restaurant that served fine Louisiana cuisine. That night, they went back to his house. They just talked and listened to music the rest of the night. The next day, Christina had a new perspective. She had a new theme song, Irreplaceable by Beyonce.

Christina reflected on her weekend with Damon. She realized that Damon had done more for her in that short weekend than Patrick had done in their entire marriage. That hit her hard. She realized that she had been settling for so much less. She knew that she was worth someone appreciating and loving her. Why did she accept that from Patrick? In the past she felt that he couldn't do any better. But the truth was, he could if he had wanted to. He never wanted to. If it wasn't something material that he could gain then why bother. That was painful for Christina.

As she begins to reflect back on their marriage, she realized that Patrick had never done anything for her. When he would buy her any kind of gift, the money always came out of the house fund. This meant that Christina paid for her own gifts to herself. She was the working spouse for most of their marriage. She always said that material things don't mean nearly as much as being treated with respect and love. She found out that Patrick was doing neither. Though very painful to realize, Christina was in the process of healing. Patrick gave Christina what she accepted from him. She accepted his lack of sacrifice. She accepted him not doing his part to financially contribute to the family. That is her responsibility in this matter. No, she did not have anything to do with Patrick's actions; however, she accepted his lack of actions. Moving forward, Christina realizes that adults must stand on their own two feet. She didn't allow family members to mooch off her then why should she allow anyone else. She decided right then that she will never allow that again.

After Christina returns home from her trip, she realizes that Patrick has been going through her email again. He tells her that he knew all about her trip with Damon. Patrick couldn't believe that Christina knew a man that cared that deeply for her. He had never heard of a Damon. He wanted her to go into detail about who Damon was. She tells him to stop invading her privacy. She goes on to tell him of her revelation after her trip. She told him that Damon had been more of a man to her in that short weekend than he had been the entire marriage. She said that he had done more for her materialistically than he had ever done for her. Patrick stood there looking like a fool. She said that's the sad truth and she accepted his nothingness. However, she says it's ok because she has learned a good lesson. Patrick realizes that Christina doesn't need or want him ever again. He feels that she thinks that he is worthless. He thinks that he'll show her. He just has to get Addison to cooperate. Then, Christina will see what she's lost. Someone does love him. She'll see that it was her and not him. Christina will see that she was the problem all along. She will come crawling back saying that the kids need their dad.

Christina would replay in her head that Patrick was pretending to go to work. He was really going around the corner to Nina's house. She feels like such a damn fool. She thinks that Patrick has been laughing at her during all of his scheming. This makes her angrier. All she can think is that this man that I have been married to for the last eight years is the enemy. When she was at her weakest after surgery, he took advantage of her. How could she ever trust him again? She knows that she can't. Christina figures that she has given Patrick her all. If she stays for that behavior, Patrick would certainly destroy her.

Samone helps Christina put things into perspective. She believes Patrick would have treated anyone he was with like this. She says that the reason he stole the money from her is because he had access. She has always thought that Patrick was such a nice guy.

She doesn't believe Patrick is laughing at her. Patrick was living his married life with her and he had his single life. He keeps everything in separate boxes. She thinks that is why he is so convincing when lying. She is sure Patrick has loved her during their marriage at some point. Samone tells Christina that she has to take the focus off him and make a plan. The plan needs to start with taking Patrick off her bank accounts.

Christina doesn't want to part with the home they had built, the suburban family life that she enjoys. The kids love their dad. This makes the decision more difficult. She doesn't know how to do shared parenting. In the end Christina realizes that her happiness needs to come first. The children are too young to understand. If she is to continue to be the best person and mother, there is only one solution.

Christina had to learn to make tough decisions at a very early age. When she was 16, she had to make the decision to have her mother come off the machines at the hospital. That decision has been with her ever since. One thing kept her sane afterwards. The fact that her mother had told her if she ever went to the hospital, never let her live on machines. From time to time she would hear amazing stories of someone waking up out of a comma after months or years. Whenever she questions whether she made the right decision, she reverts back to her mother's wishes.

Christmas Eve comes and the new family goes over to Samone's home. They exchange gifts and have a good time. The kids are happy. They know that when they get home they open their gifts. Christmas Eve is a big tradition day for the family. Christina uses it to honor her mother. It was her mother's birthday. They return home and Patrick isn't there. The kids begin to open their presents that Christina had purchased.

Patrick eventually shows up about thirty minutes late. He comes in looking wide and glassy eyed reeking of alcohol. Patrick has two arms full of dollar store toys. He comes in apologizing to the kids. He is saying that he was at the airport picking up these gifts that his sister sent them. The kids are saying, "Its ok daddy." Patrick keeps saying that they have one more box coming. Christina notices that the toys are from the dollar store. She thinks he looks like a crack head that ran in the dollar store, stole an arm full of toys and ran out. She thinks that if his sister sent them toys for Christmas, wouldn't they be in a box? It's too much trying to keep up with his lies.

She gives Patrick the camcorder so that he can continue filming the kids. She is looking at him like he is crazy and pathetic. The kids are just excited about their new toys. It is nice to see the kids laughing and happy. Patrick helps them put their toys together. Afterwards, Christina heads up stairs to her bedroom.

The next day, Christina and the children travel to Chicago for Christmas and New Years. This gives Christina some time to clear her head. She needs to get away from Patrick. The kids have a great time. Patrick is calling every day asking to talk to the kids. He had never called to talk to the kids. Christina feels like this is another one of his ploys to keep himself on the kids mind. Christina is pissed because she just wants them to forget all about that grown up stuff and play with their cousins.

Patrick is pretending that he is in Ohio, lonely and working. He is actually in Detroit with his sisters giving him advice. Patrick needs to get his next meal ticket. He knows that is it over with him and Christina. Instead of trying to make his situation right, he is working on manipulating someone else. Patrick is working on consummating his relationship with Addison.

On December 31, 2007, Christina files for an online divorce. She feels better after her decision. She and the kids return home to Ohio on January 2, 2008. She knows that she has made the best decision for her and the kids.

After several days away, Christina feels more refreshed. She begins her daily prayers again. She begins to focus more on the positive outcomes. It's amazing how a person can have faith and beliefs on a daily basis. When something unpleasant comes along, those beliefs and values go out the window at least for a brief moment.

Christina is happy to have a foundation to fall back onto. Christina begins to count her many blessings. She is grateful for their kids. She went to her gynecologist for an exam. She didn't have aids or any STDs. She is grateful for her health. She is grateful that she found out sooner than later. She is grateful for her home instructional job.

In the mist of one of her emotional moments, she realizes that this is much bigger than her. She hopes that out of all of this just maybe Patrick can become a better person and man. Despite all that he has done to her, she wants better for him because of the kids.

Christina is able to sit and talk with Patrick in regards to how to move forward under the same roof. The co exist plan is that Patrick would get another job so that he can pay all the bills. This will be the first time that Patrick would be the sole provider for the family.

His airline check would continue to go into the account while Christina maintains the house hold bills. Patrick needs to have another job within 30 days. Christina explains to Patrick that she is paying most of the bills. It is urgent that he gets another job. Christina makes sure that Patrick has gas in his car and lunch for work. However, Patrick starts requesting extra cash for cigarettes and misc. No matter what Christina does she can't shake the disgusting feelings she gets when looking at Patrick.

They feud over Patrick's extra money request. Patrick decides to have is check withdrawn from the house hold all together. Patrick has worked a lot of over time hours this particular week. He doesn't leave any room for Christina to work.

When pay day comes he thinks it is a shocker for Christina. Christina doesn't trust Patrick at all so she had predicted this. She has some extra cash set aside for emergency purposes. Patrick doesn't know this. She asked him for money. She explains to him that she didn't get the opportunity to work because he was doing overtime. He tells her that he isn't giving her shit. He was saving to go to Minnesota.

CHAPTER 10

CAT AND MOUSE

Christina begins waking up at 4am so that she could go down stairs to the basement and check Patrick's cell phone. She just wants to see what else Patrick is up to. The first night she doesn't find much. The second night, she sees a message from someone that she doesn't know. The text was from a female. Christina read the text but couldn't figure out how to make the message unread. She is so nervous of being caught. She had never gone through anyone's stuff. It is then that Patrick figures out that Christina is going through his phone.

The next night he leaves his phone in his pants pocket turned off. She realizes that he is on to her. She doesn't want him to walk down stairs and catch her red handed. She lays low for a few days. When he lets his guard back down she checks it once more.

There it is- the text message that she needs to completely take the blinders off regarding Patrick. As if she hasn't experienced enough. It is a text message from his number one mistress. The text reads-"I am glad that we didn't hook up over the holidays. I would be so angry with you right now. Were you just trying to hook up with me just for your pleasure? Were you talking to me to pass the time? Then, when you got back to Ohio it was life as usual with you, your kids and your baby mama. Now you are MIA again." Christina reads the sender. The sender's name is Gusto from work.

Gusto is Patrick's best friend growing up. He was the best man in their wedding. Christina's first thought was what Gusto is gay? She comes to her senses. She realizes that Gusto's name is a cover up. Patrick had that put in his phone just in case she checks it. Christina writes the number down. She hurries back up to her bedroom for fear of being caught. Christina wants to know who this woman is. She has to lay low. She doesn't have time to figure out how to mark the message unread. She is livid. "He is such a liar. There's no way that he's going to be cheating on me with a cell phone that I pay for."

She lays in her bed trying to figure out who this woman could be. Thirty minutes later, she goes back down to the basement, takes the cell phone and throws it in the back yard. She is trying to throw the phone in the creek behind their house.

However, her aim is off and she hits the children's sand box. She is extra nervous because it is 3'o'clock a.m. and dark. She is too scary to go outside to get the phone. She waits until Patrick goes to work. Then, she will look for the phone.

Patrick wakes up later that morning looking for his phone. Christina watches as he searches really hard for his phone. He looks in his pants, in every room, in his car. She is cracking herself up laughing as she watches him search. However, she is a bit nervous praying that he doesn't go out in the back yard for a smoke. He normally walks around the backyard. Finally, Patrick approaches Christina and ask her if she has seen his phone. She answers him with a question, "why would I see your phone?" Patrick is a bit confused because it is not her character to take his phone. However, he is very suspicious because he knows that he left his phone in his pants and that Christina had been checking his phone.

Patrick finally leaves for work without his cell phone. Christina waits for about an hour before she goes out in the back yard. She searches for the phone near the sand box. She calls her best friend, sisters, and brother to tell them about her cell phone scandal. They are laughing at her so damn hard.

Christina is not use to the cat and mouse game. She even thinks it is hilarious. She feels that this is too much work. She goes to the back yard and finds the cell phone in tact. Now that she has the phone she needs to figure out what to do next.

She really wants to know who this woman is. She has to figure out how to get the information without putting the woman on the defense. First, she did a reverse look up of the phone number.

That was how she found out where Nina lived. This time the results were none. Christina thinks that this may lead to where Patrick had spent the stolen mortgage. Next, she does the unthinkable.

CHAPTER 11

DESPERATE TIMES CALL FOR DESPERATE MEASURES

She texted the woman from Patrick's cell phone "Patrick has full blown aids, I know because he gave it to me. I know that you have been involved with Patrick. You may even have children with him. You and child need to get tested-you have been warned."

She waits for a response. She hopes that she will hear something before Patrick gets home from work. One hour goes by with no response to the text message.

The house phone rings shortly after she sends the text. She looks at the caller ID. It is a call from Detroit. She doesn't answer because she knows that it is for Patrick. The home phone rings again. Christina looks and realizes that it is the same phone number calling again. Then she realizes that it is the number that she had texted. Wow, this person has her home phone number. The woman leaves a message for Patrick on the second time. "Patrick, I need you to call me, this is Addison."

Now, Christina has a name. She immediately calls the number back. Addison answers. Christina says,

"Hi, this is Christina, Patrick's wife. I need to know why you would be calling my home phone leaving a message for my husband."

"With your husband? Hold on, let me leave my office so that I can hear and talk to you better."

Christina asked Addison why she had called her home for Patrick and not his cell phone. Addison states that she has been communicating with Patrick for the last year. Most of their communication has been on the home number. Patrick is good.

He knew that both Christina and Addison work during the day. Therefore, he always made sure that he had spoken with Addison during the day before Christina came home from work. He allowed her to call him at home.

Christina came home from work after her last pregnancy. Addison knew nothing about Patrick having a new baby. Patrick explained to her that he felt it would be best if they communicated mostly through his cell phone. He said that he was having baby mama drama. From that point forward that is how he referred to Christina.

The story Patrick had given Addison was that he and Christina were the best of friends. He explained that they live together for the sake of the children. He explained that they both have their separate lives. He would tell Addison that Christina visits her man in California quite often. He felt this would make Addison more comfortable with being with him.

Patrick never told Addison that he had been married for the last 8 in half years. He only told her that he had 2 children not three. He felt that Addison would not have got back involved with him if she knew that he was married.

Addison insists that she and Patrick had not hooked up sexually within that year. Patrick has tried to get her to come to Ohio to visit him. She never felt comfortable enough. Within this time frame, Addison and her husband were having some problems. This makes it easier for her to lean on and confide in Patrick. She tells Patrick all of her husband's issues. She feels that it is finally her and Patrick's time to be together. She is in the process of getting a divorce.

Patrick has painted such a romantic picture for her. She and Patrick have planned on being together after her divorce is final. They have discussed him leaving Christina and the children to be with the love of his life-her. They have discussed how they would blend the families. Patrick had told Addison that he wants to get her pregnant. He wants to have a son with her. Addison has two daughters.

Christina explains that she and Patrick have been married for the last 8 in half years with three children. Addison says "three?" "Yes, I have a 9 month new baby boy." Addison is in a state of disbelief and shock. "Who in the hell denies their child? Ok, its makes perfect sense. He didn't tell me about his new baby because that would mean that you and he are together."

Christina explains to Addison that the only thing she needs from her is her discretion about their communication. She tells her that she had filed for an online divorce on December 31, 2007. Interesting enough the divorce has nothing to do with Addison. Ironically; the court date is set for February 14, 2008. She asked Addison if she needs some kind of witness to prove Patrick's infidelity, may she call her. Addison says, "Yes, of course you can." Christina tells Addison that she will keep her posted. Meanwhile, Addison will continue her relationship with Patrick. The objective is for Christina to get everything she needs in her divorce.

She apologizes for the aids scare text message. She tells Addison that it is not true. She just needed a way to find out who she was. Addison says, "That's fine, I understand." After this conversation, they vow each others silence.

Their next conversation, Addison tells Christina that she and Patrick have planned a week together in Orlando, Florida. It is scheduled for the end of January. This is two weeks away. Addison will be with her company all expenses paid. Patrick just had to get there. Christina is trying to figure out what excuse he is going to use to leave for an entire week. Especially, when he is still swearing his love and asking for another chance for their marriage.

Patrick breaks into Christina's email. He sees that Christina had a reverse number search for Addison on her computer. The search turned up nothing. This is why Christina had to go to the drastic aids message. She didn't know how to get this woman's name or information. She didn't want to have to figure out who Addison was like with Nina, she'd already know. When Patrick sees that the reverse look up turned up nothing he was a little confident. However, he knew that he needed some damage control. He began asking Addison if anyone had contacted her. He told Addison that he needs to know if someone calls her.

He found that Christina had been communicating with a guy she met via the internet. He decides to send the man a message letting him know that Christina is a married woman. He writes that he should leave her alone. Brandon writes back to Patrick saying that he didn't know. He apologizes and says that he will no longer communicate with her.

Brandon decided to send Christina the message that Patrick had sent him. He liked communicating with her. He thought that she should have a say in their communication. Christina was so surprised. At the same time that Patrick sent his email, Christina had sent one to him explaining her circumstances. She and Brandon chose to keep communicating. He was something to do for Christina. He had good conversation and was the male company she needed. He was online and harmless.

Patrick finds out that Brandon isn't respecting his wishes. He sends him a more aggressive email. He attacks Brandon's character. He tells him that he has heard about his kind-internet predators. He must not have any self esteem if the only way he can meet a woman is through the internet.

Brandon responds with the same kind of aggression. He tells Patrick that Christina gave him the details to their separation. He tells him that he must not have much to offer. He said that if he had something worth while to offer then his wife would not be looking for companionship via the internet.

Patrick is growing more frustrated and desperate. He tells Christina that her new internet friend is threatening him. The sad thing is that Christina trusted Brandon before Patrick. She had never even met him. She tells Patrick that he should not go through her email or anything. She told him to prove that Brandon is threatening him. Patrick didn't have any proof. He tells her that he will give her a copy of the email. She says lets go get it. When they went to his computer to look, surprise, he couldn't find it. Of course, Christina thinks that it was never there.

Brandon tells Christina that her husband doesn't want a divorce. He says that if he didn't care it wouldn't matter who she talks to or dates. He asked if they could finally meet. He wanted to take her out to the movies. They made arrangements. Christina goes to the movies to meet Brandon.

He was so impressed with her. She didn't think that he looked like the photo on the internet. He told her that was a photo from twenty years ago. Christina feels that was deceptive. They go to Steak and Shake after the movies. They kiss. Brandon was a pretty good kisser. Christina hadn't kissed Patrick in years because he smokes cigarettes.

The two part ways. They email discussing the satisfaction of meeting each other. Brandon tells her how much he enjoyed kissing her soft lips. Patrick breaks into her email again. He is so pissed. He sends Brandon an email telling him that he best look over his shoulders when kissing another man's wife. Christina can't figure out how Patrick keeps getting into her email. She has changed the password and everything. They find out that she isn't closing her browser or clearing her history. This is how Patrick was able to invade her privacy.

Patrick tells her that he knows of her little date with Brandon. He tells her to stop her boyfriend from threatening him. He gives her a copy of an email that Brandon supposedly sent. Immediately, Christina notices that the email addresses are different. She asked Brandon about it. Brandon tells her that he has only communicated with Patrick twice. He says that he sent her both emails. Christina thinks that it's a possibility that Patrick is telling the truth. She waits until Patrick goes to work.

Samone tells Christina to check Patrick's computer for the original message that Brandon sent him. When she checks his computer he has a lot of self made email addresses with Brandon's name on them. They realize that Patrick had created several email addresses through yahoo. He had created them so that he could prove to Christina that Brandon was indeed supposedly threatening him.

Christina can't believe the lengths that Patrick goes to in order to make his lie look real. What normal person does that sort of thing? She and Samone are blown away yet again.

Christina and Brandon continue to communicate and hang out from time to time. Eventually that ended with Christina finding out that Brandon wasn't who he said he was either. Christina wonders why she is attracting so many lying ass men into her life.

Addison tells Christina that Patrick had been asking her if someone had contacted her saying anything about him. She told him no. She asked, "why would anyone be calling me telling me anything about you?" Patrick explains that he is having baby mama drama. He tells her that if anyone calls her she needs to let him know. At this time Christina hadn't contacted Addison yet.

Patrick was setting the scene to cover his ass. He is afraid that Christina would call Addison and blow his cover. He thinks that he would be left with neither of them. Also, Patrick knows that if Addison tells him what Christina tells her then he can manipulate that to his advantage.

CHAPTER 12

OFF THE BENCH AND IN THE GAME

Patrick has been playing a game with these two women without their knowledge. Now, they have become active participants in the game without his knowledge. Initially, they both want to stick it to him. Christina wants her divorce so that she can become free and clear of Patrick. Christina wants Patrick to pay. She wants him to fail at life. She hopes that he turns out like his crack head brothers and cousins or homeless uncles. Maybe then Patrick will appreciate the good wife and beautiful kids he once had.

At the same time, she hopes that this family divorce will help him become a better person and finally an independent man for the children's sake. She is so torn with all of her emotions. She and Patrick had agreed to coexist for 4 months. It takes everything in her power not to pour hot grits on him. Every time she looks at him she wants him to pay.

Addison wants Christina to get everything she desires in the divorce. She wants to expose Patrick for being a liar and cheat. She wants Patrick to be busted because he is such a lying ass pig. Addison is in a very awkward position. Here she is helping Patrick's' wife out smart her boyfriend.

She is hurt as well as Christina. Considering the circumstances Addison feels that the wife status is way more important than a girlfriend. With this in mind, she feels that by helping Christina stick it to Patrick, she will be helping herself. She would want someone to help her.

She had known and dated Patrick in the past. Patrick's infidelity is not as surprising to her as it is Christina. Some say the wife is always the last to know.

Meanwhile, Patrick is moping around the house as if he is sad about their marriage. In the basement he is calling Addison every 5 minutes or so. Patrick is scrambling trying to figure out how he could swing going to Orlando. He tells Christina that he has a training to go to with his job but he wasn't sure when. He says that he had to go and he would be gone for about a week.

Christina is laughing her butt off inside. For the first time in their marriage she actually knows that Patrick is up to no damn good. But he looks so quiet and nice. The more and more Christina and Addison communicate, the more they began to trust each other. Christina realizes the reason Patrick has got away with so much mischief during their marriage. He lies with such conviction.

Believe it or not this helps Christina to stop blaming herself. She stops being so hard on herself for not being aware of Patrick's scheming and manipulation. It isn't that she is naïve and stupid. She simply trusted her husband. He totally took advantage of that trust.

Christina and Addison decided that if Patrick comes to Florida, Addison would not see him. She will tell him that her trip had been cancelled. The scheduled Orlando trip is now. Patrick can't figure out how to swing the trip. He knows that Christina is on to him in some sort of way. He decides to lay low.

Addison didn't know how she would react if she had seen Patrick. She didn't want to melt in his arms. She is a bit relieved he didn't make it. At the same time she wants to know why he has been lying to her. After all, she had shared all of her marital problems with him. She feels if Patrick would've told her that he was in a bad marriage, she could have understood that. She is in a similar situation.

The one thing that makes Addison angry is that Patrick wasn't in a bad marriage. He is just a liar and cheat. She feels foolish for getting involved with him again. Addison and Patrick have a past. They met when they were teen agers. She thinks that no matter what, at the end of the day, they will always be friends.

She thinks that eventually, Patrick is going to come clean to her with the truth. After Addison returns home from Orlando, Patrick calls her. He asked her about her trip. She tells him that she worked and went to a few of the amusement parks. He tells her that if he would have been there, she would have hardly left the hotel room. He starts telling her how he would have been sexually pleasing her like he did when they were young. Addison is thinking, "Yuck, you are such a liar." She keeps her composure. She says "oh really."

CHAPTER 13

ORLANDO SURPRISE

It is 7a.m. there is a knock on Addison's hotel room door. She is thinking who in the hell could be there. She knows that Christina had told her that Patrick was in Ohio. "Who is it?" "It's Kenny." She opens her door and asked -to what do I owe this surprise? Kenny asked her if she was alone. "Yes, of course, why do you ask?"

Kenny tells her that he was going through her stuff a few months ago. He found where she had written in her calendar. The trip was planned that Patrick would meet her there and they would be together. Kenny tells Addison that if their marriage is going to be over, he doesn't want it to be because of another man. He tells her that he wants to try to make their marriage work again. She asked him why did he wait to tell her that he knew about the trip. He said that wanted to see for himself. He wanted to see this man. He wanted her to make a decision.

This opens up the lines of communication for the two of them. By now, Addison knows that Patrick is married, that he is not a professor at a college but a simple ramp agent at an airline. Patrick does not possess everything that her husband lacks. Patrick had made it all up. She has been confiding in the wrong man for the past year. Patrick manipulated the information that Addison had given him regarding her problems with her husband to serve his own selfish needs.

She begins from the beginning. She tells her husband that she has been in an emotional relationship with Patrick for the past year. She tells him that they have phone and cyber sex. She tells him that Patrick was in Detroit during the holidays while they were there. That is when they were going to get together and have sex. She explained that Patrick was outside of her sister's house asking her if he could come in. Patrick wanted to pretend that he was a guy selling vacuum cleaning machines.

The plan was for him to wait until you left. Patrick didn't care what he had to do to see her. He just knew that he had to have sex with her. He needed to seal the deal. Patrick wanted Addison to disrespect her husband. All of Addison's family knew Patrick from the past. Kenny is the only person that wouldn't know who he was.

As a matter of fact, Addison had been telling her mom and twin sister that she and Patrick had finally made their way back to each other. She would tell them that he has finally got his life together. She would tell them that Patrick is in love with her again. After all those years, she feels the same.

In the past Addison would do anything for Patrick. She says that he just had that affect on her. Addison explains to Patrick that though she and Kenny were separated they were married. She couldn't do that to him. She tells Patrick that she would call him after Kenny leaves with his brother. She tells Patrick that she will get a hotel and call him later. He says ok, however, she goes to sleep. They never hook up. Patrick kept calling her that night. By the time she awakens and calls him back he didn't have any transportation. Patrick is pissed that he didn't get to have sex with her that night. At this time Patrick is really catching the blues from Christina. He wanted something to work out for him. It didn't matter who got hurt in the process.

"You would have done that to me?" Addison says that she did think about it. She reminds Kenny that they are and had been separated for the last year. She doesn't feel that she was cheating on him because they had decided they were getting a divorce. They could date whomever they wanted while they were separated.

She had been lonely. Patrick contacts her. He is like a breath of fresh air. He is familiar and safe. Patrick seems to be a great father, provider, and all around good man. She really believed that Patrick had finally got himself together.

He is her first love and sexual partner. As a young girl she loved Patrick more than she loved herself. Her parents didn't like her with him because they observed that too. You know that when one is young and in love, she will do anything. When ones parents express a dislike for the guy, it just makes him more irresistible. She thought that it was finally time for the two of them to be together.

She wants full disclosure to Kenny. She feels that if they are going to work on their marriage, it was important for her to be honest about Patrick. She tells him that she has just recently found out that her relationship with Patrick is one big lie. Patrick is married. She has been calling his home. She feels that Patrick is the same liar and cheat that he was when they were young.

She explains to him that she had spoken to Patrick's wife Christina. They had an in-depth conversation. They are just watching Patrick's actions and taking notes. Christina may need to contact her again to testify to Patrick's infidelity if needed. Kenny says that Patrick is pretty bold to have had her calling his home. Kenny is not happy with Addison's involvement with Patrick. He is a bit relieved that Addison had found out that he is married. Patrick is not this perfect man. They agree to move forward and to work on their marriage.

Addison calls Christina right after her husband leaves Florida. She tells Christina of their discussion. She tells her how grateful she is to have spoken to her prior to going to Florida. She says that if Patrick had been there when her husband came it would have been a bad situation. She would've lost her husband forever for lying ass Patrick. She would have been none the wiser about Patrick.

Christina says "no- thank you. If someone would have bet me one million dollars that my husband Patrick was doing any of the things I have found out about in the last 6 months, I would have lost a million dollars."

"Oh girl, I could have told you that his ass was a cheat. That's all he did when we were together. I would see Patrick out and about years ago, always hugged up on some woman. I never suspected that he was married. Whenever we would see each other we would hook up. I really didn't think he was married after this holiday season. We were on the phone twenty-four/seven. I thought that if he was with his baby's mama then wouldn't he be with his family."

CHAPTER 14

ADDISON BACKGROUND

Addison was born in Michigan. She is the youngest of seven children. She has a twin sister. She is from a financially well to do family. Her mother is a professor at a university. Her father owns several McDonalds. She was raised in suburban Michigan. She has grown up in the church. She sings in the choir. Her parents involved her in all types of pageants when she was young. Basically, Addison grew up in a very sheltered life. She is very family oriented and has enjoyed many of the finer things in life. She hasn't had to struggle much at all.

She met Patrick when she was 15 years old at the skating rink. Patrick as we know by know is from the streets of Detroit. They were introduced by a mutual friend. They began dating. Patrick told Addison that he loved her. He said that he wanted to show her by having sex before he went off to college. Addison was a virgin. Patrick was not, however, he told Addison that he was a virgin.

She decided to have sex with Patrick because she loved him. She wanted him to remember her while he was away in college. Addison was in high school. Afterwards, she spent the next several years loving and wanting Patrick. Patrick went away to college. He was doing what college freshmen do which is party. He tried getting as many girls in bed as possible. Addison was back in Michigan love sick.

She was sending him gifts and money. Anything he asked for she would get it from her parents. Her parents didn't like or approve of Patrick for her. They thought that he was up to no good. They felt that he was a user. Parents can sense these things regardless of how humble of a person Patrick seemed.

Addison would often make her self sick because she wanted to be with him so badly. The more her parents disliked and disapproved of him, the more she was drawn to him. Her parents found out that she had lost her virginity to Patrick. They were not pleased. Soon after, she found out that Patrick had been cheating on her with another girl that went to his high school. He took this girl to his high school prom. The only way she found out was because she saw the pictures in his senior book.

Her parents would not allow Patrick to take her to her school prom. She was escorted by her friend Mario. Her parents just didn't trust Patrick. They didn't want their daughter getting pregnant as a teen. Her parents felt that she loved Patrick more than herself. Patrick had this control over Addison. Often, she would catch him in lies and confront him. He would always have his two sisters call her and ask to give him another chance. Without fail they came to his rescue. Time and time again. It didn't matter whether he was right or wrong or how bad he had hurt her. They would call her and say that the two of them belong together. She needs to forgive him because he loves her.

It wasn't until Addison went off to college in Atlanta that she was finally able to concentrate on herself. She learned what she liked and disliked. She began to come into her own. However, Patrick was her first love and he knew it. He would often resurface, usually asking if he could borrow some money. He always had a sob story. She always bought it.

For the first two years of her college experience, she and Patrick were talking on the phone and writing letters. By this time Patrick had dropped out of college and was back in Detroit. He would tell her that he wanted her to have a baby for him. He would even ask her about her cycle. He would tell her that he had done research. He knew when the best time was to get her pregnant. He told her that he was in love with her and wanted to marry her. All this time, he was living with his girlfriend from college. He and Nikki started dating in Florida. They both were from the Motor City. When she graduated, she and Patrick left Florida and returned to Detroit together.

Addison's parents were furious when they discovered that she had been talking to Patrick every night. Their phone bill was ridiculous. She would get in trouble every month but that didn't stop her from talking to Patrick. He would often go missing in action. When he would find out that she was coming home he would get in touch with her.

The good thing about Patrick going missing is that Addison would continue living the college life. She began to get more dating experience. It started to dawn on her that Patrick wasn't that good for her. But he always had this way of making her want to be with him. That young love is wonderful. Sometimes it's innocent and sometimes not.

Patrick knew that Addison got a monthly allowance from her family in undergrad and grad school. Her undergrad allowance was $3000 per month. Her graduate allowance was $5000 per month. Patrick would call for money more often than not.

Addison found out that Patrick had been dating and living with another woman all the while. That gave her a major dose of reality. She stopped giving him loans that he never paid back. She stopped talking to him for awhile.

She began to love herself more. She dated different guys. She pledged a sorority (pink and green). She just totally started to enjoy the college experience without Patrick. She got on with her life. She began dating a childhood friend-Kenny.

Addison and her boyfriend now husband Kenny had two girls while in college. Her parents got nannies for them so that they could finish their studies. They moved in together. Afterwards, they both finished grad school. They moved back to Michigan. Addison's parents love Kenny. They have known him since he was a young boy.

Patrick reenters the scene once they return to Michigan. He and Addison would occasionally hook up for sex. They would get together whenever they saw each other. It didn't matter who either of them were dating at the time. When Kenny and Addison were dating he found out about Patrick. Patrick would not stop calling her.

One day, Patrick called Addison's apartment and Kenny answered the phone. The two of them had some words. Basically, Kenny told Patrick to get fucking lost. He said that they were together and he is the father of her children. Patrick got angry with Addison. He couldn't believe that she had let Kenny come between them.

Patrick moves on to be with his live in girlfriend Nikki. The communication ceased for that moment in time. Addison has always had a soft spot for Patrick. Regardless of what Kenny had told Patrick, that didn't cease.

CHAPTER 15

SLEEPING WITH THE ENEMY

Christina is finally beginning to understand what it means to be a product of your environment. She knows that Patrick is from a dysfunctional family. She always thought that he was one of the good ones. Though the people he associated himself with were no good, she thought he was better. It turns out that because she thought he was good he portrayed that to her. Unfortunately, when a person tries to be someone else, it never lasts long. A person's true identity is always revealed. In most cases this happens later than sooner. A lot of damage has been done.

Christina is afraid of Patrick. She doesn't know what he was capable of doing. She began to watch him through Addison. It is amazing. He would be down stairs in her basement talking to Addison. He would be having phone sex. He is confessing his love for her. All the while, he is coming up to Christina's bedroom asking her for another chance. He didn't look any different. He looks and acts so sincere. Christina was thoroughly disgusted by even the sight of him.

At this point, Christina and Addison are on the phone while Patrick is home. They are comparing notes. This helps Christina realize how she had missed seeing all of Patrick's mischief in the past. Hell, he is good. He is good because she trusted him.

Many times when men lie, cheat, and get away, it is because of a trust that women have for them. Once women catch on to the game, they are much smarter. He has become very predictable. Whenever they compare notes, they find that Patrick is lying about everything. It is like he creates completely new versions of the situations. For example, if Patrick had hamburgers and fries for dinner, he would say that he had steak and lobster.

Christina and Addison have been in communication now for about three weeks. However, it didn't become real for Addison until one day she was on the phone with Christina. Patrick enters Christina's room trying to discuss the initial divorce proceedings. Addison is in disbelief. It all connects for her at that moment. The two decide that it would be best to keep their communication to themselves indefinitely. They both began to think that Patrick is unstable. Addison tells Christina that she doesn't want Patrick to do any harm to her and the kids.

Christina begins sleeping with her bedroom door locked. She puts a hamper next to it. This way, if Patrick unlocks her door and comes in at least she would hear the door hit the hamper. She sleeps with her purse under her pillow. She has all of the children to sleep in the room with her. One night Patrick enters her room. The door hits the hamper and awakens her. She wants to know why in the hell is he in her bedroom. He is pissed that the hamper had given him away. He makes up some story about needing something in her bathroom. She explains to him once again that he is not allowed in her room.

Initially, the kids would be down stairs in the basement with Patrick. He begins telling them that he had done a bad thing and that's why they are getting a divorce. He begins to cry and so do the kids. The kids begin to feel sorry for Patrick. He begins to use that to his advantage. He tells the kids that they need to help him work on a plan to get their parents back together. Who manipulates their children in that way? Christina thinks that is even lower than stealing the family's mortgage.

Patrick brings the new born baby to Christina's room during the night for nursing. Christina finds out from her daughter that the baby is always crying when he is down stairs with Patrick. This outrages Christina. The one thing she doesn't like is her baby crying for his mommy. Patrick knows this but he doesn't want to be down stairs in the basement alone.

He starts working on their 7 year old son. He tells him lies about his mother. This is causing problems with Christina and her 7 year old son. He is beginning to have animosity for her. She knows that she needs to break this hold that Patrick has on him. Therefore, she tells the kids they can visit with their dad in the basement but they all will sleep up stairs.

Christina explains to her children that there should be no secrets. She tells them no matter who it is request them to keep a secret from their mommy they should not. They can harm them. They should not keep secrets from their mommy ever. The kids said ok. Christina doesn't know how to deal with this. She simply tells Patrick to leave the children out of grown up business. He has the nerve to say that the kids are coming to him trying to keep the two of them married.

One night in particular, Patrick enters Christina's room. He is butt ass naked from his waist down. His dick is at attention. He gives Christina the baby for nursing. Patrick is horny. He is thinking that if he hasn't had sex with Christina then she must be horny too. He feels that if she sees his hard dick then she may want it. He thinks that they can call truths long enough for him to bust a nut.

Christina is not interested. As a matter of fact, he scares her. When she doesn't respond in the manner he hopes, he goes back down stairs to the basement. Christina isn't comfortable with the entire situation. Her oldest son is left in the basement with Patrick. Ten minutes later, Christina goes to get her son.

When she goes to the basement, Patrick is laying on the air mattress with their son. Christina just picks him up and carries him up stairs to her bedroom. She is not sure what Patrick is capable of doing. She wants to know why in the hell was Patrick lying with their son. She doesn't think that was appropriate especially, after he had just left her bedroom naked with a hard dick.

It is 3 am. Christina can't sleep after this. Christina calls Addison. She tells her what just happened. They talk for awhile. Addison is awake because she had just got off the phone having phone sex with Patrick. They figure he had got aroused with Addison. He was hoping to release his energy into Christina. She can't believe this guy. He actually thought that she would want him. Afterwards, Christina settles back down and is able to go back to sleep.

The next morning, Christina sees Patrick in the kitchen. Initially, she thinks that she shouldn't mention it. Then she decides to let him know that what he did last night was totally inappropriate. Patrick responds by asking her what is she talking about. She says do you need me to spell it out for you. Patrick says yes because he has no idea what she is talking about. She explains to him that coming into her bedroom naked waist down is unacceptable. He says "naked waist down, what are you talking about? I wasn't naked. I had my underwear on." Christina is baffled. "Are you serious?"

Aggressively, he says that he didn't do that. He is so convincing that if Christina hadn't called Addison right after it happened, she may have thought that she dreamed it. Christina chuckles and says- "ok I see I made the whole thing up. Is that what you are telling me?" Patrick says "yeah, I guess you are." Then he says he had on his underwear and maybe his dick happened to fall out.

Christina calls Addison. She tells her how Patrick responded when she confronted him. She tells her that if she hadn't called her right when it happened that he would have almost convinced her that she is crazy. They really start to believe that he is unstable. Who lies like that and gets angry when he is called on it.

Christina calls her brother to tell him about the whole situation. Her brother starts to laugh. "Wow, that guy is confused. He is lying and scheming so much that he doesn't know whether he is coming or going. You two wouldn't be playing me like that, I would have been figured something out but not Patrick."

Patrick had loyalty from both these women in the past. He never would suspect that they would be smart enough to betray him. They are both honest and trustworthy. However, they are pistols when you piss them off. Therefore, Patrick figures if they ever talked, one of them would confront him. This would give him the advantage he needs to work it out with both of them. If he knows what each of them know then he tells them what they want to hear. The two of them have very similar personalities. Patrick would try to convince them that the other is lying on him. He would tell each of them that the other is jealous because he chose her.

CHAPTER 16

DMV

Christina and Patrick have to go to the DMV to transfer tags and titles of their vehicles into the appropriate owner's name. Christina has to pay for everything as usual. Patrick's broke ass don't have any money. Christina is furious. All she could think to herself is to punch him in the fucking face.

"What made you steal all of my money? You must have been laughing at me the entire time. You were making a fool out of me. You were saying that you were working leaving the house at 1 a.m. You were going around the corner to Nina's house for a sex rendezvous. You must be laughing on the inside because I am continuing to pay your way."

He sits there looking stupid as hell. He tells her that he doesn't know what he was thinking. He says that he isn't laughing at her. The more he talks the more she wants to punch him in his face. This was the first time the two have been alone without the children since Addison hit the scene. Patrick and Christina have never had a physical altercation.

Christina feels like she is having an outer body experience. She has to move away from him in the DMV. She knows that if she hits him in there, then, she would have to go to jail. All Christina can think about is the Ike and Tina Turner scene. She feels this is about to be them.

Patrick has done so much damage. Everyone is hurting but him. Christina, the children and Addison are all victims. Instead of trying to do right he is continuing to lie and get over. Christina feels that anyone else would have hurt Patrick long before now.

As they leave the DMV, all hell breaks out. They get into the car. Christina just can't control her impulse any longer. When they sat in the car, she says, "I just want to fight you." Before she could get the word fight out her mouth, she had reached over and punched him in his face. Then, she punches him again. She is screaming, "you bastard, how could you?" He grabs her hands and clinches his fist preparing to hit her back. She tells him, "You go ahead mother fucker." Then, she bites his hands so that he would let her go. When he does, she punches his ass in the face once more. She tells him that's the very least his loser ass deserves. He yells at her to take him home.

She drives home. However, she starts to think of consequences for her actions. She isn't sure how unstable Patrick is. She doesn't want him to get back at her by doing something to the children. She begins to think of damage control. However, she knows that Patrick would try and use it to his advantage. Shortly after they get to the house, she goes down to the basement. She asked if she could have a moment to speak with him.

He agrees. She begins by apologizing. She says that she couldn't believe that she lost control in that way. She tells him that she is glad that he didn't hit her back. He says that is the least that he deserved. He takes this opportunity to tell her that he wishes that was all it took for them to get back together. He walks up rubbing and grinding on her. The nerve of this guy. He thinks that he is about to get some pussy. She runs off up stairs telling him sex was never a problem for her. She tells him that nothing has changed between the two of them. She was very theatrical.

She tells her sister and friends about what had happened. They all say- good, it is about damn time. They feel that is the least he deserves. They think that she should have knocked the shit out of him long before now. She calls Addison. Addison actually feels a little sorry for Patrick. However, she tells her that she would've been knocked the hell out of him. She doesn't know how Christina can even look at him let alone live with him without punching him. They agree that the damage control is needed. They continue to feel that he is unstable.

Addison and Christina begin talking on the phone almost every day after the first divorce day fiasco. The online divorce company didn't prepare the paperwork properly so the judge wouldn't see them. The nerve of Patrick to say that it is a sign that they shouldn't get divorced. This is when Christina decides to get an attorney. This is one of her smarter moves. This means that Christina needs Addison a little while longer. It is so ironic. Addison is actually Christina's counsel during this entire time. Eventually, the roles flip flop. Addison loves Patrick. However, she can't help but to think that Christina loves him as well. She feels that Christina is his wife and the mother of his children. Her feelings are more important in this situation. She is able to put aside her relationship with Patrick at least for the moment.

CHAPTER 17

ADDISON'S FRIEND RANA CALLS

Things really began to escalate after the DMV. Patrick realizes Christina doesn't want him. He begins talking to Addison about 10 times a day. He is always arranging to meet her somewhere. She is stringing him along until the divorce is final. She and Christina talk almost daily. They are predicting his every move. Patrick decides that he is going to visit Addison in Minnesota. He says that he just had to see her. He tells her that he hadn't had sex in 10 months. He only wants to be with her.

He keeps telling her that he needs her to pay for a place for him to stay when he gets there. She asked why she should pay for him a place. He tells her that he is paying for a second airline ticket. The first time he wanted to see her, he lost money on that ticket. He feels that she should pay him back. Remember, Patrick works at an airline so he doesn't have to pay for his tickets. He is trying to hustle her out of some money.

Everyday Patrick speaks with Addison. He tells her these elaborate stories about going to teach classes at the university. He tells her that he is over exhibits that never existed. He tells her that the noise she hears in the background is construction. He explains that they are expanding the campus. He doesn't want her to be alarmed. He would be walking on campus heading to and from class.

Christina and Addison are killing themselves with laughter. They can't believe that one would go through such lengths. The funny thing is that Patrick would just make up stories and experiences based on being a college professor. It is so deep that he tells Addison that he has slept with a few of his students. He says it wasn't until they were out of his class.

At this point, Patrick believes that Addison has no idea about him being married to Christina. His story is that Christina is his two baby's mama. He had explained to Addison that they had been having a few issues as of late. He never would go into detail. Patrick begins to pour it on really thick for Addison. Addison is amused because she has known Patrick for many years. Patrick had never pursued her so strongly. He has never opened up much about anything. He has always been quiet and held back on information. She finds this very interesting.

Rana calls Addison yelling and cursing saying "I told you that bastard is no good! I just found out that Patrick is married to Christina and has three children. The guy I'm dating is friends with Patrick. He didn't know that Patrick was stepping out on his family. He was just talking and let it out. He feels bad because he thinks that he has caused some trouble for Patrick." Addison calmly tells Rana that she knows. She explains to her that she and Christina have been in communication. Rana continues to tell Addison that Patrick has never been any good for her.

Addison and Christina discuss this new discovery. They decide to use it to their advantage. They predict that Rana's boyfriend would get in contact with Patrick. They also predict that Patrick would try to come clean before Rana tells Addison that he is married. Sure enough, Patrick starts calling Addison saying that he really needs to talk to her. He has some things that he needs to get off his chest. He needs to be honest about something before they move any further. Addison decides that she won't take any of his calls for a few days. This is a very good situation for Christina and Addison. This way Patrick would never have to know that the two of them were in cahoots. He would think that Rana told her that he was married.

During this time Patrick is working over time at the airport. He is planning his trip to Minnesota. He decides to take his check from the house and keep it all for himself. He didn't tell Christina of this until it happened. Patrick tells Christina that he would do what he wants with his check. He decides that he isn't going to pay any bills. He tells Christina that he is not moving out.

If she wants utilities paid then she would have to do it. Christina predicted that he would do this, so she was prepared. She pretends to be surprised and hurt. She tells Patrick that she has no money. The kids need things. She explained to him that she hasn't been able to work because he was working overtime. There is no one to watch the kids. He says, so what does that have to do with me? Christina has always split everything with Patrick. He is showing his true self. Christina feels that he is a monster. She doesn't know this man.

She reminds him that they have a coexisting agreement. She says that he needs to give her some of that money until she can get some things figured out. He says that he isn't giving her anything and he doesn't. Christina takes the kids to Chicago to be with her family for awhile. Patrick goes to the airport to assist with the kids. The entire time Patrick is biting his lip and rocking his knee. He had always done that in the past, Christina just thought it was some kind of nervous condition.

Christina gets to the airport and accidently leaves her purse on the shuttle. Patrick arrives. She discovers that her purse is missing. Patrick volunteers to go find it. She knows that she can't let that happen. Patrick would have stolen her money and said he found it that way. He would have discovered that Christina and Addison had been talking with each other for a very long time. If he discovers this, their gig would be up. Christina needs her divorce.

Christina leaves Patrick with the children. She calls the shuttle company. The driver had discovered it right away. Within fifteen minutes she has her purse returned to her with everything in tact. Christina calls Addison to talk about this entire scenario. They both breathe a sigh of relief.

Since Patrick claims that he came to help with the children, she left them with him. She walks through the airport talking to Addison. Addison is telling her how Patrick is blowing up her phone. Christina tells Addison that maybe he does love her. If she wants to be with him, she would be fine with that. Addison says that she couldn't do that even if she wants to because that would be betrayal. She explains to her that if Patrick could treat his wife and kids that bad, then why would he treat her any differently. Addison feels that Patrick is trying to line up his next meal ticket. Christina and the kids depart for Chicago.

Addison finally answers Patrick's call. He tells her that he is married but about to be divorced. He knew that her friend Rana had already told her. He says that he is sorry. He didn't tell her because he didn't want to lose her. He says that he thinks that they should see each other to talk this out. He asked if he could come to Minnesota anyway. She tells him that it would be a waste of time. She calls him a liar. She tells him that he has hurt her for the last time.

Patrick confesses to her that he has been unhappy his entire marriage. He tells her that he is finally divorcing Christina because she is frivolous with money. He says that she doesn't know how to run her household. He explains that Christina doesn't like his family and vice versa. He goes on to say that he should have been married to her. He wished they had kids together. He explains to Addison that he has always cheated on Christina with his ex girlfriend Nikki. He says that he always had different women because Christina wasn't her. The reason he has been so unhappy is because he is with the wrong woman. He married Christina because she was pregnant. He did what was right for his children. He says that he has never loved Christina. Christina wasn't pregnant when she and Patrick married. He is trying to appear honorable. He is lying again. Addison is amazed at the amount of information that Patrick is giving up.

Now, that the cat is out of the bag regarding Patrick and Christina being married, Patrick begins to speak more openly about Christina. He references her as his wife. Finally, Addison says "why is every word out of your mouth my wife this, my wife that?" Patrick says that he is just so use to calling her that. "Well that's strange because the entire year that we have been communicating you didn't let it out once." Patrick says "ok, I didn't tell you because I was unhappy."

Addison says, "I was having problems in my marriage as well. However, I told you that I was married and the problems that I was having. Not only were you married but you have a third child with your wife. She was pregnant the entire time that we were talking. You never mentioned anything. I gave you ample opportunities to be honest. Do you even know what it means to be honest?"

Patrick is catching it from both ends now. He is trying to work through this with Addison. He is hoping that she will eventually forgive him and give him another chance. Patrick needs to make sure they are together. After all, he has told everyone that he is finally with the love of his life. Patrick needs another woman to take care of him. The truth is that Patrick has never taken care of himself.

Addison isn't getting the treatment from Patrick that Christina is getting. She is getting the nice guy. The guy that loves her and wants to spend the rest of his life with her. She is getting Dr. Patrick. She is getting the father of the year. She is hoping that eventually Patrick is going to come clean with her about everything. She believes that at the end of the day she and Patrick are at least friends. After all, they have known each other since they were teens.

Patrick tells Addison that he is coming to Minnesota to visit her. He says that if he has to sit in the airport all day and night until he sees her then that's what he will do. He says that he isn't going to let Christina ruin their relationship. Addison finally says ok. Patrick asked Addison if she can have her company pay for his hotel. "Sure Patrick anything for you." Patrick gets on the next flight to Minnesota.

Patrick arrives in Minnesota. He calls and calls Addison's cell phone but get no answer. Finally, he begins to call her home. Addison doesn't want Kenny to answer the phone. By this time she and her husband are back together. They have been living together again for about one month. She finally answers her home phone. Patrick tells her that he is in Minnesota. He wants to know what hotel she had got for him. Addison tells him that she didn't. He tells her that he can understand that she's upset but he needs a place to stay. "That isn't my problem. I told you that coming to Minnesota would be a waste of your time."

He calls her the next day. He asked if they can please have lunch. He tells her that he wants to see her. She doesn't respond. He leaves her a message telling her that his wife had cancelled his credit card. He needs some money to pay for his room. He begs her to come and just help him out this one time. She ignores that message. Finally, after two days without seeing her, he tells her that he is flying back home to Ohio.

Out of curiosity, she goes to see him before his flight leaves. She is quite disappointed. Patrick had told her that he looks as good now as when he was a teen ager. When she sees him, she thinks that he is skinny. She is disgusted with his brown teeth that came from years of cigarette smoking. She doesn't know this man. He doesn't look the same. There is something dark about him.

Patrick seems to be happy to see Addison. He is pissed that he had spent his own money for a hotel. He is especially pissed that he didn't get to have sex with Addison.

He is very self conscious. He wants to know if she is satisfied with the way he looks. He tells her that she looks good enough to eat. He says that she doesn't look like she has two babies. He boards his flight back to Ohio with much disappointment and frustration. Addison and Christina are tickled pink. That's what his lying ass deserves.

Christina asked Addison if she was disappointed because she knows he is a liar and cheat. She wants to know if Addison would have been attracted to him if they had never communicated. Addison says that she probably would have looked past the physical characteristics because she is in love with him. She says that initially she would have been disappointed. She would have been able to eventually get past it. They move forward. Patrick is angry. He goes back to Ohio and takes his frustrations out on Christina. She is prepared because she knows how his trip went.

CHAPTER 18

PREPARING TO VACATE

Christina has been packing, boxing, and labeling everything she plans to take. She is throwing things away. Samone and Rita are laughing at her. They are saying that it is too early. Christina explains when it's time she will be ready. Patrick is looking at Christina as if she isn't serious. He has little hope that she is going to change her mind. After all, it isn't going as well as he hopes with Addison. He is angry from the Minnesota trip.

He often starts little brush fire arguments with Christina. For example, he tells her that he doesn't want her to take the curtains. He has never cared about any damn curtains in the 8 years they have been married. Christina would simply say that she is not having this conversation with him.

By now, Patrick is becoming increasingly frustrated. Neither Christina nor Addison has any respect for him. He is being beaten at his own game. The fact is he doesn't know it. After Patrick decides to take his check, Christina tells him that he should not use anything in the house. She tells him that since he is not paying anything then he can't use it. She tells him that he should not eat her food. If he doesn't touch any of her belongings everything would be fine. She explains to him that he needs to help cook for the kids or take them out.

He says he is not going to take them out to eat with him. He can't afford it. Christina is pissed. She tells him that when he was on her dollar he and the kids stayed at a restaurant. He says "so what, I can't afford to take them out and I won't." Patrick realizes that it is more difficult to eat out everyday, pay for his own gas, and pay for hotel rooms in Minnesota. He ran out of money fast. When he ran out of money, he decided that he's going to take whatever he wants in the house. He doesn't care that he didn't give Christina any money for anything.

Christina wants to reserve conflict as much as possible. Rita and Samone tell her not worry about Patrick eating her food and using any of her things. They tell her that he wants to beat her anyway because things weren't going in his favor with anything. Against their advice, Christina confronts Patrick about eating the food she bought. She reminds him that he had taken his check from the house months ago. The kids are sitting having dinner and watching television.

Christina whispers to Patrick that she wants him to put her food down. He tells her that he isn't putting a damn thing down. He is going to eat her food whether she likes it or not. She attempts to grab the plate from Patrick. He slams the plate into her chest and pushes her down on the floor. The kids are scared. They start crying. Christina gets up very angry. She doesn't want her kids to see anything like this.

She throws the cordless phone at the wall in frustration. Patrick picks the phone up and throws it at her as hard as he could. He is cursing calling her bitches and fools. Christina calls 911 and explains that her husband is attacking her in front of her kids. Patrick rushes her, takes the phone and hangs it up. He throws the phone to the floor and bust it up. He's yelling that he is going to kill her.

She rushes the children up stairs. She gets them in her bedroom. She goes to a place where she has a pistol. Patrick had purchased a gun and left it in the basement on the pool table. She had put it away for safety. She put the kids in the closet and tells them not to come out. They know that she has a gun. They are terrified. They have never witnessed anything like this. Patrick stays down stairs cursing for a few more minutes. Then he leaves because he knows the police are on their way. Christina calls Rita and tells her to come over right away. Christina has the gun but she doesn't want to use it. However, she is not going to allow Patrick to harm her or do anything that will take her away from her children.

The police arrive shortly. They take her statement. She tells them that he hit her on the foot with the cordless phone. She doesn't have a bruise so they can't pick him up. They tell her that she has to go down to the courthouse to press charges. "Where is Patrick?" She tells them that he had left because he knew they were coming. The police leave their home. They park at the end of the street.

As Rita arrives, Patrick is coming down the street. He sees the police and turns around. Christina notifies the police that it is Patrick. The police stop his vehicle. Christina gives Rita a brief summary of what happened. She shows her the gun. Rita has never seen Christina in any kind of domestic situation. She wants Patrick to go away.

The police escort Patrick back to the property to get some things. Patrick tells the police that he wants to retrieve his gun. The police asked for the weapon. Rita doesn't want to give it to the officer. She feels they would give it to Patrick. Christina turns the gun over to the officers. The police take the gun to the station. It is not registered.

Patrick has given the police a completely different story. This time there is a male and female officer. Patrick says that Christina attacked him. Patrick agrees to leave for the night so that things can simmer down. Christina calls her brother. Wesley tells her that Patrick has shown no regards for her long before now. He explains that now he has no regards for the children. "The coexisting arrangement is a failure. It is over. You should not spend one more night under the same roof."

Christina and Rita have plans to whip Patrick's ass if he shows back up to the house. The next morning, Addison calls Christina. She asked if she was ok. She has talked to Patrick. He is sounding really crazy. He tells Addison that Christina attacked him in front of their children. Christina tells Addison the story and explains that she and her sister are ready to fuck him up when he gets there. Addison suggested to Christina that she should take the kids to a friend's house. That way they won't have to experience anything traumatic again. Christina agrees.

Christina calls one of the moving companies in her address book. She had previously got quotes from them in preparation for their move. She takes the kids to her friend's home. The movers are there in and out within two hours. They had a cancellation that morning. Therefore, they were able to move her. Addison tells her that she would be talking to Patrick. She said that she will let her know when he is on his way there. Christina thanks her and hangs up the phone.

Wesley calls Christina to get Patrick's cell phone number. He calls Patrick and tells him that there will be problems if he ever touches his sister again. Patrick tells him that he didn't touch her; if he had the police would have taken him to jail. Wesley simply says if you touch her again you won't have to worry about the police. Addison is keeping Christina in the know regarding Patrick's whereabouts and actions.

Christina has their belongings taken to the garage in the apartment community where she plans to move. Christina and Rita visit two weekly hotels. The first one is on the same side of town they live. Christina is very disappointed with the up keep of this place. The manager tells her about the second one which is on the completely other side of town. She likes this one much better. She knows it will only be for about one month.

By the time Patrick gets to their home, everything and everyone is gone. It is for the best. This way no altercations could take place. No one gets physically harmed.

Christina goes to the courthouse to file chargers on Patrick for the previous night. To her surprise Patrick shows up at the same place. Rita is waiting in the van parked outside of the courthouse. He scares her because he pulls in front of the van yelling, "Where are my children?" Rita calls Christina to tell her that Patrick is at the courthouse.

Christina is in the process of giving her statement. Sure enough, another case worker enters the room. He whispers to Christina's case worker. The case worker explains to Christina that her spouse is in the lobby filing a report on her. Afterwards, he escorts her out of the employee elevator so that Patrick doesn't see her. Patrick thinks that he is going to see her exit the building.

She gets into the car. She tells Rita how they let her out the back. Rita tells Christina that she doesn't trust Addison. She thinks that Addison told Patrick where they were going. Christina says that she doesn't believe that Addison would do that. Rita asked her to explain how Patrick knew where they were. She tells Rita that she thinks that Patrick was coming to press charges on her and saw the van. She says that she is sure that the officers told Patrick the same thing they told her about pressing charges. She explains to Rita that Addison doesn't have a reason to betray her in that way. Rita says neither did Patrick but we see how that is turning out.

Addison calls asking if all is okay. She says that Patrick told her that he was going down to the police station to pick up his gun. In all actuality he was going downtown to press charges on Christina. The crazy thing with Patrick is that he lies about everything. You really don't know what is true unless you have proof. Christina asked Addison if she mentioned anything to Patrick regarding them going to the courthouse. She says, "of course not."

She calls Patrick on three way- so that Christina can hear what he is saying. Patrick is talking so incredibly nice to Addison. It makes Christina want to puke. Addison asked him if he is sure that he didn't do anything to Christina that would make her afraid of him. Patrick says in his nicest voice "no, you know I wouldn't do anything like that." She probes a little longer and they get off the phone. Christina is satisfied with trusting Addison. The two of them understand their situation is quite unorthodox. They both know that the only people that need to understand their relationship is them.

They go to pick up the kids. They take Rita home. Christina and the kids go to the hotel and get settle. She explains to them that they are going to be there temporarily. She tells them they will not be seeing or talking to their dad for awhile. Things need to settle down. She says that once things settle down then they will make some type of shared parenting arrangement. They are there for two days. Christina's bankruptcy discharged and they move into their apartment.

In the meanwhile, Patrick has gone home to Detroit. Addison keeps Christina informed on what Patrick is planning next. She calls and tells her that Patrick is in Detroit so if she needs anything else from the house, then she should go get it. Patrick sisters tell him that he should change the locks. How funny is that? Patrick has been stealing the mortgage that Christina was paying. They tell him to change the locks. Patrick is there for about two weeks. When he is on his way back, Addison lets Christina know.

Christina doesn't respond to any of Patrick's calls or text messages the entire time. The only thing he does while he is in Detroit is drank and go to strip clubs with Arny. He is talking to Addison as his confidante. In his mind, she is his woman.

Patrick asked Addison to marry him. He tells her that they should move to Florida together. He wants them to begin a new life together. She is the woman that he should have been sharing his life with all this time. He doesn't want to waste any more time. He wants them to start their life right away. She sees that Patrick is living in another dimension. However, she is planning on how to get rid of him.

Christina doesn't like the fact that Patrick thinks he has Addison during this process. She wants him to suffer. It doesn't seem like he is because he thinks that he is with her. But at the same time she needs to know what he is planning. She wants to know what he is up to at all times. Patrick sisters are advising him on how to handle Christina.

In the meantime, Patrick decides to pay Rana a visit. He wanted Rana to tell him everything that she told Addison. He is telling Rana that he loves Addison. He wants Rana to call her back to tell her how much he loves her. Rana feels sorry for him. He is sitting on her sofa looking like he wants to cry. He tells Rana that he is not mad at her for telling Addison. He pleads with her to say that he doesn't love his wife, he loves Addison. Rana calls Addison. She tells her of the visit. She actually felt sorry for Patrick. He convinced Rana that Addison is the love of his life. He was going to leave Christina. Christina and Addison are amazed at how easily Patrick can get others to buy into his lies. Patrick never tells Addison that he visited her friend Rana.

CHAPTER 19

PATRICK'S PLAN

The truth is that Patrick had no plans of leaving Christina and the kids. He was going to wait until Addison divorced Kenny. Then he would do double duty as Christina's husband and Addison's man. He figured that since Addison has money, she would get him an apartment in Minnesota. He would tell Christina that he has training to advance in the industry. He had plans to tell her that his trainings are twice a month. He was going to say that he would be gone between 3-4 days per training.

With this plan he could show Addison how much he loves her. He would tell her that he really wants to be with her. The only problem is that he can't leave his kids. He would explain that this would be the only way they could be together. Patrick would not have to lose Christina but would also have the so called love of his life. He wouldn't have to pay for anything. He works at the airline so his flights are free. Addison would provide food, shelter and transportation. He figures his plan would be perfect. Christina trusts Patrick; therefore, he knew that he could get away with it for at least a little while.

Patrick knows that if Addison found out that he has been lying, he would still have Christina and the kids. Remember, Christina is the bread winner and provider for him in Ohio. He would be living the life. Patrick has been bragging to all of his family and friends about his situation. He just needs to seal the deal. He needs Addison to get divorced so that he can have that control of the entire situation.

Patrick figured that he could begin to treat Christina anyway he wanted because he has some where else to live. He becomes very arrogant. He stops doing things around the house. He isn't cutting the grass. He isn't taking care of basic maintenance of the home. He begins going out after work.

Patrick would have his cake and eat it too. He is so full of himself. He thinks Christina is such a fool. She thinks that she is so intelligent. He would often think to himself. She is actually the biggest dummy that I have ever been with. He has been stealing money from Christina since they had been married. She never ever suspected him. He knows that he can get Addison to trust him that completely as well. He just needs that damn Mario or Kenny out of the way.

He tells his friends and family that he is so unhappy with Christina. He says that the only reason he is still with her is because of the kids. Christina is totally oblivious to all of this. She thought they were living a very happy married life. Patrick would often times tell her how happy he is to be married to her. He would tell her that he has always loved her from the moment they met in college.

Patrick needs to make himself appear acceptable to his friends and family. He needs to have a reason for cheating on Christina. Patrick knew that his sisters believed that Christina is a no nonsense type of girl. She makes decisions that are best for her and her family. She doesn't care what people think. They don't like the fact that she has that type of attitude. They think that she is arrogant.

Prior to Patrick and Christina marrying, they would have Patrick do whatever they needed. He was their little brother. They took care of his shelter and money. They were always bailing him out of any kind of situation he found himself in. If he didn't pay his rent he would be put out. They would allow him to live with him. He always told them that someone had wronged him. He would borrow money from them and never pay it back. Then, he would act like it was no big deal. He acts like someone just gave his grown ass the money. They have enabled him all of his life. He has never been a man that has taken responsibility for his actions.

Unfortunately, Christina doesn't realize this until it is too late. She simply picked up taking care of Patrick where his sisters had left off. However, Patrick sisters have known him long enough to know their brother. They want to believe that all of the accomplishments that Christina and Patrick have made after they married are somehow due to Patrick turning over a new lease on life.

They want to believe that Patrick is the bread winner. They want to believe that he is miraculously responsible. Patrick tells them that he is responsible for all of their accomplishments. They know that Patrick has never accomplished much on his own. As a matter of fact, they can't tell you anything he has done on his own since he has become an adult. Other than marry a good woman. They compliment him on helping raise his children as if it is an option.

Based on the way Patrick was raised he feels that helping out with his children is an option. The truth is Patrick has no respect for women. He hates his mom because she was an alcoholic. In turn he treated his mom the way he saw his dad treat her- disrespectfully. Patrick's dad is an alcoholic but for some reason it is more horrid for the mother to be a drunk. Patrick and his sisters basically praise their dad. They fought with their mom until she died a murderous death. She was killed by one of his sister's nephews. His sister is married to the murderer's uncle. The husband's nephew killed Patrick's mom. Even after that, they blamed her for trusting a drug addict.

After it all began to unravel, Patrick begins telling his sisters of his plan to be with Addison. He tells them that Christina is bitter because he wants Addison. But Patrick knows that Christina is done with him. He needs to make sure that his sisters don't contact Christina. He needs to make them as angry with her as he is. He needs for her to look bad and not him. He knows that Christina would spill the beans. He knows that she wouldn't mention Addison. He knows that afterwards, they would begin questioning him. He doesn't need or want that from his sisters. At this time Christina had left the home and cut communication with Patrick for approximately 3 weeks.

He needs their support. He wants them to take care of him. He knows if they have a clue then they wouldn't feel sorry for him.

Deep down, his sisters know that Patrick is Patrick. The same brother they have always known. He's just resurfacing. He looks so mature and responsible as a husband and a father. He is losing his legitimacy.

It doesn't help that the sister's husbands are telling them that Patrick isn't telling the entire truth. They have known lying ass Patrick for a long time. They know all Patrick does is lie but they never felt that it was that important. They learned not to loan him any money. They too were feeling sorry for Patrick. Christina is the villain because after all she took his kids away. It doesn't matter that Patrick attacked her. Remember, Patrick's story is that she attacked him and he defended himself. Christina married into the family, so naturally they would take his side. It doesn't matter whether he is lying or telling the truth. They feel sorry for him. They pick up taking care of Patrick like they always had.

For weeks Patrick parades back and forth from Michigan to Ohio. He pretends that he is keeping their home. He goes back and forth until people stop giving him money. They stop allowing him to mooch off of them. Not long, he is back in Michigan for good. All of the utilities are shut off at their old home due to lack of payment. At this time Patrick isn't paying child support. He has no reason not to have taken care of his living expenses.

He lives with his sister Kim for a while. His niece moves into a house and he moves in with her. Now, he is there mooching off her. He tells everyone that they are buying her house together. He tells her that he can't pay his portion of the bills because Christina is getting it all in child support. Patrick preys on women because men make you pay your own way. Men only feel sorry for you for a couple of days. After that, you've got to come up off some money to support yourself. If you can't support yourself then that is your own problem.

His niece told her mom and dad about her experiences living with Patrick. Patrick is summoned to a meeting at their home. Her parents tell Patrick that he has to find his own place to live.

CHAPTER 20

CALLING IN REINFORCEMENTS

By now, Patrick realizes that he needs help with Addison. He calls in reinforcement. Patrick has his sister Cindy call Addison. She tells Addison that Patrick has been unhappy in his marriage for a long time. She tells Addison that she really thinks that it is time for her and Patrick to be together. They need to start praying and going to church together. She says that Patrick has always loved her. Addison is amazed that after all of these years they are still covering for him. Addison just listens. She wanders what makes them think that she wants to be a part of a family like theirs.

Patrick has his dad talk to Addison on the phone. Patrick's dad gets on the phone and tells her that the two of them are meant to be together. They need to stop playing around and have him some grandchildren. Patrick asked his secretly bi sexual boyfriend Arny to get on the phone. He tells Addison that Patrick loves her. He says that Patrick had settled for Christina. That is the reason he is in this mess now.

Patrick has his friend Louis call Addison. He leaves several messages for her. He tells her that he wants to speak to her on Patrick's behalf. She thinks this is funny. She doesn't know him personally. Why did he think he could talk to her? All she knows about Louis is that his wife cheated on him with a friend. How is he going to help them. He can't control his own wife. Patrick is pulling all of the stops to get back in her good graces.

At this moment they realize that Patrick has told his family that he is divorcing Christina for Addison. Addison overhears Patrick and Kim talking. He tells her that his marriage is over. He tells her that Christina didn't know about Addison until now. He says that he tried to work things out with Christina but he has always been in love with Addison. Kim tells him that he and Addison

89

are meant to be. She tells Patrick that he needs to be honest with Addison. He says that he is trying to be honest. She is upset with him for not telling her that he is married. She tells him to give her a little time and she will come around.

Patrick and Addison are constantly on the phone. She tells him that she can't be with him anymore. She has to stop talking to him. He is crying saying that he can't lose her right now. He doesn't know what he will do. He's giving her his sob story that Christina has taken the kids and he doesn't know where they are. His sister walks in while he is crying to Addison. She thinks that it is Christina. "Give me that phone, so that I can tell her a thing or two." "This isn't Christina on the phone, it's Addison." "Oh, tell her hi for me."

Even though the information from Addison to Christina is bitter sweet, Christina loves being a few steps ahead of Patrick.

CHAPTER 21

ADDISON IS WITH MARIO

Addison concocts a story that she is with Mario. Mario is an entertainer. He and Addison grew up together. He took Addison to her high school prom because her parents wouldn't allow Patrick to take her. They have a history. They are best friends. Not even Kenny knows how close the two of them are. Addison needs a way to get rid of Patrick after he and Christina are divorced. Patrick is clinging to Addison now more than ever. Christina and the kids have moved out. Patrick is begging Addison to come visit him. Addison doesn't want Patrick to know that she and Kenny are back together. She doesn't want him to cause any drama in her home. The idea is to break free of Patrick without any more damage.

Patrick finds out that Mario is performing at a Detroit casino. He and a couple of his boys go there. Patrick tells them that he wants to go for a little gambling. Patrick finds the VIP room that Mario and his crew are partying. He manages to talk himself into the area. Mario happens to recognize Patrick because he keeps walking by him staring. Addison has not told Mario of her story that they are together.

Just so happens, Mario calls Addison and says, "Hey, you remember that little dude you said was your boyfriend back in the day? I think that I see him. He keeps walking by me staring."

"OMG! Listen Mario, if he ask you if we are together tell him yes. It's a long story. I need you to cover and I will explain everything later."

Mario chooses to be sly and asked "what's in it for me?" and starts to laugh.

"Whatever you want, please do this for me." He says ok. Sure enough Patrick approaches Mario. Mario's body guard blocks Patrick from coming near Mario.

"Hey man, do you remember me? I am friends with Addison." Mario allows his body guard to let him come in. "What's up man, what can I do for you?" Patrick replies with "do you mind if I have a word with you?" Patrick asked if his boys can come into his VIP room. Mario says sure. Mario tells them to help themselves to free drinks and food. They are excited to have a free night out. They think that they are getting perks because Patrick is dating Addison.

Patrick begins to tell Mario that he has a wife and children. He tells him that he has always cheated on his wife. Mario says "ok, but what does that have to do with me." Patrick proceeds to say that he is and has always been in love with Addison. He tells Mario that Addison told him they are together and fucking. Mario almost swallowed a piece of ice when Patrick said fucking. Mario tells Patrick that it's true. He says that he and Addison are together.

He tells Patrick that the difference between himself and Patrick is that Addison returns his love. Mario explains that Addison is with him. Patrick tells Mario that he has all this wealth, fame, and women to choose from. He goes on to say, "Why can't you let me have Addison?"

Mario thinks that Patrick is a punk. After all, who comes to another man asking him if he can have his woman? Patrick thinks that Mario would have some compassion for his love for Addison. Mario tells Patrick that he and Addison are going to be together. He says "so what I have fame and fortune. Addison wants to be with me not you." Patrick says, "I know I am just asking if you could step aside and not stand in the way of our chance for happiness." Mario is thinking that this dude is crazy. Mario says one more time in no uncertain terms that Addison is with him.

As a matter a fact, we will be in New York together next week. Patrick set back on the sofa and starts to cry. After Patrick gathers himself, he and his boys leave the VIP room. Mario can't wait to call Addison. He says "what in the hell is wrong with him. He acts like a bitch. What have you done to that little guy?" Addison explains a summary of what is going on. Mario is just laughing. Patrick never mentions this event to Addison. This shows Addison how much more scandalous Patrick actually can be. Addison calls Christina and tells her of this drama. They both say- unbelievable.

CHAPTER 22

SHARED PARENTING ULTAMADOMS

Christina finally accepts a call from Patrick. They agree to meet in a public place to discuss parenting arrangements. Patrick returns to Ohio. He doesn't know that Christina knew he was in Detroit. Patrick is proclaiming that he did nothing wrong. He insists that Christina is the cause of their problems. He is angry that Christina was able to free herself of him so quickly. He didn't see it coming. He assumed that she had no money to make a move so abruptly.

He notices that Christina had returned to their home and retrieved more things. He can't figure out how Christina is out maneuvering him. How did she know that he wasn't there? Maybe the neighbors are telling her. Even so, she wouldn't know when he would return. Why wasn't she scared to get caught?

Christina is so disgusted by the mere sight of Patrick. They agree to put the children first. They agree on visitation. Now, Patrick and Christina have a shared parenting agreement. Patrick has the kids by day. This gives Christina the opportunity to work. Christina has the kids from the evening on. Patrick works the evening shift. This agreement allows for the kids to continue to be home schooled. Everyone can work and make a living for themselves. The children get to experience quality time with both parents. This is the plan. However, Christina begins to enjoy her time just a little too much for Patrick's satisfaction.

He begins to make it tougher on Christina. He starts working more over time. She isn't allowed to work unless she pays someone to watch the kids. She argues with Patrick that it is his responsibility to pay for childcare. It is his time with the kids. Patrick disagrees and tells her that he isn't paying anything. He is being such an asshole.

She feels that Patrick is jeopardizing her livelihood. She makes appointments with students based on her shared parenting schedule. Patrick thinks that Christina is at his mercy. He feels that she needs him. He's very angry with her. He is disappointed with his relationship with Addison.

When he does get the kids he is always late. He calls Christina to bring them back to her before the scheduled time. He starts arguments with her if she isn't home. This is stressing Christina out. She doesn't quite know how to handle this person. He looks like the man she was married to but behaves totally different.

Usually, she would have no interaction with a person like this. The law mandates that she cooperates with him because of the children. How does a mother handle this difficult situation? The interesting point to make here is that Patrick thinks that he is justified in what he is doing to Christina. He is trying to have her fail. He wants her to regret her decision to leave him. He doesn't want her to succeed because then it looks like she doesn't need him.

However, he knows that Christina has never failed at anything. He doesn't want to look like he is the loser in all of this. Things aren't going as he planned with Addison. He is lying about Christina to his family and friends. He is such a good liar that he convinces himself that it is true. Christina tells Patrick that he must be crazy if he thinks that he can have a healthy relationship with the kids by being disrespectful to her. He tells her that one thing has nothing to do with the other.

Christina enjoys her time to focus on herself. She's able to do some things she wants when Patrick has the kids. However, his drama is getting to be way too much for her. Patrick is so unreliable. She can't make any plans because she is not sure if he will or will not show to pick up the kids. Christina weighs her pros and cons.

Christina goes out on a date with a pilot. He takes her out for a flight lesson and dinner. She is enjoying herself until Patrick starts calling her. He's saying that he is bringing the kids home.

She tells him that she is out. She reminds him that she has 3 more hours. He tells her he has something to do. He always says that he is called into work (mandatory). Christina explains to Patrick that she has worked at the airline. She had never been called in for mandatory work. That only time that happens is when you are already at work.

Patrick threatens that if she doesn't come and get the kids then he will leave them in the car at the airport parking lot. Patrick knows that he will get her attention with that statement.

"If you do you will surely go to jail for child abuse." Patrick figures she is on a date. He starts calling every five minutes. Her date asked if she needs to leave. He tells her that she should be careful with Patrick. He seems angry or crazy to keep calling like that. Christina ends the date early. Needless to say, she never hears from that guy again. Patrick scares him off with his drama.

When she gets to their old home to get the kids, they are outside. It is 9pm. The kids get into her van. Patrick tells Christina that he hopes the guy she was with was worth it. He calls her a stupid ass bitch. She can't believe this mother fucker. She loses all of her cool. She tells him that his dead cut throat ass mother is the stupid ass bitch. She closes her car door.

Patrick backs his car into her van. The kids are scared. She tells them that she is going to have to call the police on their dad if her door is dented. She drives off because she doesn't want the kids to witness any more foolishness. When she gets home, she checks the door. It was not dented.

The next day Patrick calls her as if nothing has happened. He apologizes for his behavior. Christina tells him that his behavior is not acceptable. She says that calling her a bitch and hitting her car should have landed him in jail. He is lucky that he didn't damage it. By now, Christina is almost at her wits end with Patrick. She has been trying to separate Patrick's behavior towards her from being the kid's daddy. It is becoming increasingly difficult.

Later on that same week, Patrick has the kids. He attempts to bring them back early again. Christina is out again. She explains to him that he is unfair. She has made plans and she will not be there. He tells her if she doesn't come home by 10pm then he would take them to meet someone.

Christina almost lost her mind. She calls her aunt in Chicago to tell her what is going on. Her aunt advises her not to respond to Patrick. He has been using the children to keep her in control and upset. Patrick knows that Christina would respond to something like that. He knows that she is very protective of her children.

Christina doesn't respond. Patrick brings the kids home at about 5am. She answers the door and let her kids into their home. Patrick has the nerve to try and argue with Christina telling her that she isn't right. Christina simply closes her door and takes her kids to bed.

The final straw for Christina is when Patrick is to get the kids for the weekend. Christina has made plans to go out of town. Patrick tells her that she needs to wash clothes for them. He says that she needs to send food for them. She tells him that it is his responsibility to do those things while they are with him. He tells her if she doesn't then he will not watch them. He says, "better yet I will watch them; However, your kids will be over here hungry and dirty."

That's it. She is done dealing with this loser. She makes the decision to take Patrick out of the equation. She stops answering her home phone. Patrick is calling all times day and night. Christina realizes that she no longer needs her home phone. She has it disconnected.

He is texting her. She has text messaging removed from her cell phone. Once she begins taking care of the children completely on her own, she could exhale. It is difficult but she doesn't have to worry about stranger danger Patrick. He is such a wild card. She hopes he will go and jump off a building.

He isn't working much so she is getting only $200 per month for three children. She hates him. It is bad enough that he turns out to be a terrible husband. It makes her sick when she thinks of him as a dad. The kids did nothing wrong. Patrick acts like he loves them so much until he has to be responsible for them. The kids don't see Patrick acting this way. This angers Christina because it looks like she is keeping the children from their dad. She looks like she is always mad at Patrick for no reason.

Patrick starts showing up at the kids bowling and basketball games. He knows when they play because their schedule was set prior to Christina distancing her self from him. He doesn't help pay for anything. Yet, he shows up with the nerve to tell the kids how to play. If there is ever a time to vomit.

She can't stand the fact that he is there as if he is still apart of their family. He is acting like he has something to do with their success. He doesn't even bring the kids a bottle of water. She thinks he is so pathetic.

However, the kids love their dad. They don't know much about all that grown up stuff. All they know is that they like seeing him. That pisses Christina off because here she is busting her ass raising them alone. It seems like he gets as much love from them as she does. She feels that this is unfair. She feels that Patrick doesn't deserve their love. She often lashes out at them after Patrick leaves. Soon after, she apologizes to them. She tries to explain why she gets so angry. The kids forgive her and they move forward.

This drama goes on for about three months or more. Christina realizes that Patrick getting the children is more trouble than it is worth. The children would hear the two of them arguing about why he can't pick them up. The kids loved their old neighborhood. They enjoy playing with their friends. Christina finds out that Patrick is not supervising them when they are there. She received two phone calls from former neighbors. They were calling to tell her that her baby boy is outside alone in his stroller while the kids are playing. Christina goes ballistic. She tells Patrick that she doesn't accept him endangering her children.

Patrick begins to go missing in action. Christina finds out that Patrick was getting the children attempting to avoid paying child support. When that strategy didn't work, he stops cooperating all together.

Finally, Patrick has been put out of their old home. He was not paying the bills. The ceiling in the kitchen came down. There was a leak somewhere and he didn't have it fixed. Christina enters the house to get the children's bikes. She can't believe how one person can cause so much damage to a house. Patrick claims that he moved out because he couldn't afford the monthly bills and mortgage. Christina is reminded that this fool says he couldn't afford it but he was stealing her mortgage. She nick named him loser boy. He moves back to Detroit soon after.

CHAPTER 23

PORNO PATRICK

Patrick is becoming very sexually explicit. Whenever he talks to Addison, the conversation revolves around sex. He begins emailing and texting her photos of his dick. He sends her videos of himself ejaculating. She asked him to stop. He completely ignores her. He sends her taped videos of himself imaging that he is having sex with her. He is talking dirty. It is actually quite hilarious.

Addison and Christina discuss his behavior. Christina tells Addison that she has never seen this side of Patrick. Addison decides to share the photos and videos. After all, it is her husband. They are laughing their asses off. Everyday for two months, Patrick photos himself and shares with Addison. She then shares with Christina. Christina then shares with her sisters. They are all having one big ass laugh. They are emailing jokes for each photo.

Christina thinks that it's nasty. She points out how skinny he looks in the photos. Christina is not the least bit turned on by the photos. However, she thinks that it could be sexy if it is from someone she likes. Addison thinks that Patrick is trying to get sexual attention. He wants her to desire him. He hopes that he can make her feel the way he did so many years ago. She finds this funny because she's had so many different partners since Patrick.

Patrick thinks that if she sees what she's missing then she will want it. Addison tells Christina that he has never been so aggressive. They think that maybe he's not getting as much sex since he and Christina split. He no longer has access to Christina's finances so he can't impress other women to sleep with him. It cost to date.

Christina asked Addison why would he keep sending the photos if you are telling him to stop. Addison says that he is delusional. He is living in the past. Christina asked Addison if she believes that Patrick really loves her. "I believe that he believes that he loves me. We have had phone and cybersex. That's why he feels it's a turn on. He thinks the only reason I'm not responsive to it now is because I am angry with him. I am angry because he has been married our entire relationship. I became emotionally in love with him. The only thing left to do was fuck. I have always let Patrick come back. He feels this is no different. It is going to take a little more time."

There are times when Patrick had the children. He calls Addison for cybersex. She tells him how inappropriate it is. The kids could walk in on him. He says they are outside. This confirms the accusations from two former neighbors that the kids were unsupervised when with Patrick. Christina gets frustrated with Patrick. She knows that he is not supervising the kids but she can't reveal her source.

It's so funny because when Christina says something that only he and Addison should know it shocks him. He would ask Addison if she has been showing anyone the pictures he sends her. She and Addison have one more laugh. She tells Patrick in no uncertain terms that he needs to stop sending her photos. He tells her that if she loves him, she would be doing the same thing. He asked her why is she all of the sudden so high and mighty. Why does she think that she is better than him? She says that's just it, "I don't love you." He tells her that she did before she found out that he was married. He says that no matter what, love doesn't just go away.

CHAPTER 24

MEMORIAL DAY WEEKEND

Christina is enjoying her new found freedoms. She has her own space and loving it. She hasn't spoken to Addison in a few weeks. She figures that Patrick has probably stopped chasing her so desperately. Christina decides to call Addison just to see what she has been doing. Basically, she is checking in on her.

Addison tells Christina that she and her family were in Detroit for an annual cook out. Her brother- in- law is a radio personality in Detroit. Therefore, each year they attend the Memorial Day Festivities at Belle Island. All of Addison and Kenny's family were in attendance. This year they acquire uninvited guests. Patrick and Arny show up to her family's function. It's a public place so anyone can be there.

Addison's family knows Patrick from when they were young. Patrick remembers that they always meet this time of year. He decides to go and confess his everlasting love for Addison. Patrick has assumed that Addison had not told Kenny about their relationship. He wants to blow Addison out of the water. He wants to cause problems between her and Kenny. He knows that if he goes Kenny would be in the dark. However, he is the one in the dark. Remember, Addison opened up to Kenny about Patrick in Orlando.

Patrick begins to make a scene. Initially, he goes to Addison's grand mom. He tells her how much he loves Addison. He says that she is destined to be with him and not Kenny. Addison's grand mom is sad for Patrick. He looks like this nice love struck young man. He looks like he is hurting so much because Addison is reunited with Kenny. Patrick believes that the only reason Addison went back to Kenny is because she found out that he was married all the while they were communicating.

Patrick feels that if he can only cause a fall out between the two of them, Addison would run back to him.

Addison can not believe that Patrick is at her husband's family gathering. She thinks that he is disrespectful. After all, her children are there. After he sees that the only thing that grand mom can offer is sympathy, Patrick confronts Kenny. He's wearing a baseball jersey, jeans and church shoes. Clearly, he looks hot and bothered. Arny is telling Patrick to lets leave. Arny looks surprised that Patrick is confronting Kenny.

Patrick tells Kenny that Addison loves him. He says that he can't stand by without fighting for his woman. He tells Kenny that their marriage is a joke. Patrick is embarrassing himself. Kenny wants to kick Patrick's ass. He has to keep his composure because his daughters are looking. By now, everyone in the vicinity is watching.

Kenny's family are all ready to whip both Patrick and Arny's ass. Patrick didn't tell Arny specifically why he wanted to go to Belle Isle that day. He told him that he wanted to go pick up some women. Arny is upset with Patrick because he feels Patrick has put him in danger. Arny gets Patrick to leave before things get really ugly.

Kenny is upset. Addison is relieved she came clean about Patrick in Orlando. They talk about what needs to be done about Patrick. They discuss having a restraining order put out against him. Kenny's brother says that he would have to pose some type of danger for the police to do that. They decide to block Patrick's cell number from their home phone. They talk about Addison getting a new cell phone. That wasn't an option; she has had that number for 11 years. All of her business and personal is done with that number.

Kenny is angry. He wants to know why Addison has still been communicating with Patrick. She tries to explain their plan involving Christina's divorce. Addison calls Christina and asked her to talk to Kenny. She wanted her to explain their plan. Kenny agrees to speak with Christina. He says okay, he hopes they know what they are doing. He wants this situation over. He wants Patrick out of their lives before someone gets hurt. They have Patrick's cell number blocked from their home phone. Patrick is relentless. He calls from another phone. This time Kenny answers the phone. Patrick apologizes for the scene he caused. Kenny tells Patrick in no uncertain terms that he has no respect for him. He tells him to stay the hell away from his family. He says if he comes near them again it won't be so pleasant.

Patrick asked Kenny if that was a threat. Kenny said no that is a promise. Patrick tells Kenny that he will not be bothering them again. He was just calling to apologize. Addison walks in while they are finishing the conversation. Needless to say, he didn't stop there.

The next time Patrick contacts her, she tells him that if he doesn't stop harassing her, she will file a restraining order against him. He says that he is showing his love. He hasn't done anything to her but love her. He wants to know what is her problem.

"My problem, you ask. You show up uninvited to my husband's family event. You show no regard for me or my family. You only care about what you want. It doesn't matter who gets hurt in the process. You're a liar. It's no wonder your wife left your ass! My advice to you is to try to fix your marriage and leave me the hell alone." Patrick angrily hangs up on Addison. Later that day, he sends her another picture text of himself ejaculating. His text reads, "Can I lick your asshole?" Clearly he didn't get the right message.

CHAPTER 25

DAY OF DIVORCE

The day of the divorce hearing was full of uncertainties. Patrick had pretended that he wasn't aware of the date. He agreed to keep the children. Christina had been praying that he didn't show up because she wants it over and done. Patrick signed all of the papers months prior to the date. Christina persuaded Addison to call and whisper sweet nothings in his ear. The purpose was to remind him of what he would be gaining. If he did come to court, he would want it over as well. Otherwise, he would have to explain to Addison why it wasn't over.

Come to find out Patrick had already been down to the court house with the children. Patrick calls Christina as she is pulling into a parking space at the courthouse. He tells her that the court date is today. She asked why he had her kids down at the courthouse. He claims that he had some other business to handle there. He decided to check in on the divorce date. She tells him that she is at work in a meeting with her supervisor. She will have her attorney reschedule. He says ok untrustingly.

He expresses to Christina that there are some things in the papers that he just doesn't agree with anymore; therefore he wants to be at the court proceedings. She is not happy. However, he did leave the courthouse. She goes into the courthouse to meet with her attorney. Rita is her witness, who just happens to be late. Christina is really nervous because she wants to be free. They had gone to a previous hearing without an attorney. The case was dismissed because the paper work wasn't completed correctly.

Christina is really nervous. She begins to think that it is impossible to get this divorce done without Patrick's presence. She can't believe that her sister is late. Her attorney advises her to calm down. "It is ok that Rita is running a little late. We have a 30 minute grace period." Eventually Rita arrives. "You know how important this is for me. I am always here for you when you need me." Christina is frustrated with Patrick having the kids at the courthouse. She feels that he is trying to pull something scandalous involving the children. She finally takes her attorney's advice, exhales and relaxes.

One thing Patrick doesn't know is that he doesn't have to be present for the divorce to be final. He thinks that he will have one final word. He is trying to use Christina's attorney for his benefit. What is he thinking? Christina wasn't going to tell him when the court date was. He received the paperwork. The divorce would have happened anyway because he had signed all of the necessary papers.

Christina explains to her attorney that Patrick is at the court house with their children. Her attorney advises her to tell him that the court hearing is today. The attorney doesn't want any complications that will give the judge a reason to reschedule. In other words, she doesn't want Patrick to go to the courthouse after they leave and make any false accusations.

Christina calls Patrick informing him that she is at the court house. "The hearing will be today." Then, she tells him that he doesn't have to be there. He yells at her saying that he wants to be there. He keeps repeating that he no longer agrees with the paper work.

She tells him that she doesn't want her kids at the court house. He tells her that is too bad because they are here. Christina is upset. She knows that Patrick was getting the kids half the time so that he could claim joint custody. He was informed that if he got joint custody, he wouldn't have to pay child support.

Patrick and the kids come to the third floor of the court house. Now that Patrick is there Christina doesn't need a witness. Rita is able to watch the kids. They go before the judge. To no surprise Patrick says that he no longer agrees with the papers. The judge tells him that he has up to 3 years to get an attorney. The thought of being married to Patrick 3 more years sends Christina into a rage. She begins to cry calling him a liar, cheat and thief. She cries, "Why won't you just let me free?" Patrick looks embarrassed. As usual, he appears to be the sane and rational one. Christina's outburst doesn't help matters. The judge tells Christina to be quiet so that Patrick can speak.

The attorney advises Christina to simmer down. She tells her that the guards put unruly people in jail. She advises Christina to drop the alimony. This way Patrick would agree to the terms and the divorce can be over today. Christina doesn't want to do that. She feels that Patrick is going to get away with no consequence for stealing her money. She doesn't think that it is fair for him to do all of the damage and walk away without a scratch. She knows that peace of mind is priceless. After all, the money is already gone. It is the principal.

Patrick thinks that he doesn't have to pay child support until the divorce is final. After all, they have been living separate for 4 months. He hasn't paid anything. The attorney explains to him that she is filing a child support order to begin immediately. Regardless to the divorce becoming final today. Patrick has told all of his family that he is divorcing Christina so that he can be with the love of his life Addison.

Patrick begins to rethink postponing the divorce. The truth is Christina has no respect for Patrick. He knows that there is no getting back together. She can't stand the sight of him. He thinks he will show her by getting with Addison. He believes that Addison is waiting to be with him. She loves him and she has plenty of money to support him. He'll show Christina that someone worthy wants to be with him. When he gets with Addison, Christina will be the one looking stupid. She will regret divorcing him.

The attorney says that she doesn't care who Patrick gets to represent him. She will win. However, she advises her that it would be better and cheaper to get it over now. The attorney asked Patrick and Christina to come into a conference room. She asked Patrick what it will take to get this over today. Patrick thinks that he is in the driver's seat now.

"For starters I will pay something in child support but I don't make that much money. I can't afford to pay $100 per child." The attorney tells Patrick that the courts make the adjustment. "The courts can't take more than 50% of his pay." He goes on to say that he doesn't want to pay Christina alimony. Christina is disgusted. She tells him that it is just called alimony. They had agreed that Patrick would pay her money back and it would be in the form of alimony. He sits there and tries to argue that because they were married it was his money too. The attorney asked if he worked and earned the money that he took. Patrick said no. "He just pretended to work."

"The truth is that it was Christina's money. How much can you afford to pay back monthly?"

"I don't know maybe $100."Christina quickly says "I will take it. Now, lets get this over and done."

The attorney is acting as a mediator between the two. She asked Christina to be quiet and allow her to do her job. She asked Patrick if he is comfortable enough to get it over today. He agreed. The judge agrees to see them again. The judge asked them if they agree and want to be divorced. Christina says yes. Patrick responds with a sarcastic please. They both walk out of the court room.

Christina is happy. Patrick looks defeated. Christina thanks Patrick for getting the divorce over today. The kids go home with Christina because Patrick had to go to work. Christina is ecstatic. She is happy to be legally free of Patrick.

She knows that Patrick would eventually fall off with helping with the kids. The truth is that before Christina married Patrick and began taking care of him, his sisters took care of him. Christina is hoping that Patrick is going to step into manhood and independence for the kid's sake. Patrick is hoping to work things out with Addison.

Christina calls Samone, who has been waiting on pins and needles. "It's over," they both say thank God.

"We have to celebrate." Christina tells her it will have to wait until next week. She gets on the airplane. She travels to Florida for a little birthday celebration of her own. She calls Addison and expresses her gratitude for all that she has done to help support and protect her and the kids. Christina recaps how the day went in court. Addison is happy for Christina. Now, she needs to figure out how to get Patrick out of her life for good.

CHAPTER 26

ROLE REVERSAL
ADDISON EMOTIONS

Interesting turn of events, Christina begins to become more removed from the situation. She is so happy to have her own living space. She is able to let go of much of the tension that had built up from months of living with this SOCIOPATH. They begin to deal with Addison's emotions in all of this. Christina and Addison had become so cool that they communicate about Patrick like old girlfriends. Christina realizes that Addison had fallen back in love with Patrick. Christina was so caught up in her own emotions early on that she didn't see that. Christina says to Addison "OMG, you fell back in love with him."

Addison admits it. She tells Christina that she didn't admit it earlier because she feels so stupid. She knows how much of a liar and cheat Patrick had been in the past. She didn't want to admit that she had fallen for it again. She can't believe that she was going to divorce her husband and be with Patrick.

She admits that she has always loved Patrick. She wishes that Patrick was Kenny. She thought that she and Patrick were meant to be together. She thinks that Patrick does love her. She believed that he was going to leave Christina and the children to be with her. She says that is why she would have paid for Patrick a car and apartment. She felt that if he loved her that much then that would be the least that she could do for him.

That conversation opens the door for the healing to begin. The first step to overcoming any type of addiction is honesty with yourself. It's so amazing. Christina is so removed. It's like Addison is talking about someone Christina doesn't know.

Addison begins to tell Christina stories of their past. The funny thing is that the more stories Addison tells the more she understands why she and Patrick were not together. Patrick has always been a user, liar and cheat in her book. He has never done anything for her. She was always giving. She would talk about how they would send each other love letters when he was in college.

Patrick talks to Addison as if she should just get over his lies. He has valid reasons why he was lying. He tells her he wants to come clean with her about everything. He writes her a letter. Addison calls Christina telling her that Patrick is finally about to tell the truth. She tells her that she will call her once the letter gets to her. Addison gets the letter and reads it. She calls Christina and reads it to her. She laughs her butt off because Patrick is just continuing to lie. She and Christina didn't even have to trust each other. All they had to do was tell a story and Patrick's would always be different. It had got to a point where Patrick was telling lies about the lies he had previously told.

When the letter didn't work, he sends her a taped confession via a web cam. In his confession, he says that the only thing he has lied to her about is working for the airline. He tells her that he works for the airline so that the kids are able to travel for free. They play travel league sports and it cuts the fees down tremendously. He says that he did tell her that he was married, she doesn't remember. He says that he didn't lie about his third child, he simply didn't tell her about him. He says that he is a professor at Columbus College. He gives her a web site to check his name listed on their web page. Literally, Patrick tells a lie every time he opens his mouth. The sad thing is he is continuing to lie. He isn't an professor at a college. He just lies and doesn't expect anyone to check on it.

Patrick tells Addison that he wants to prove to her that he and Christina are over. He tells her he wants the two of them to meet. That way they can begin to merge their families. He expects Addison to say no. Addison says, "That is a perfect idea. I would love to meet the mother of your children." Patrick is stunned.

Addison calls Christina to tell her that funny ass joke. They both laugh. Christina says, "I would like to see that fool come to me with that foolishness." He returns to Addison the next day and says that Christina said "no, she doesn't want to meet no bitch that he is fucking." They both have yet another laugh at this lying ass fool.

CHAPTER 27

ADDISON AND KENNY MOVING FORWARD

Addison and Kenny renew their vows. They have a private ceremony with only family. They agree to refocus their energy on their family. They decide they want to have more children. Addison had to be persuaded. After all, she has been a career woman for the last 13 years. The thought of becoming a new mother again is overwhelming. They have a major issue. Addison had her tubes tied years ago. They need to determine what direction to take. Instead of having a surgery to undo, they choose Envetro (artificial impregnation). The procedure is very uncomfortable. She hopes that it is a success the first time. She doesn't know if she can go through with the doctors removing her eggs again. The procedure is successful. Addison is officially pregnant.

Their families are extremely excited. She wanted to keep it secret at least until the first trimester. She calls that the safety zone. Her twin sister went to the doctor with her. She tells their mom. It spread like a wild fire from there. This would be the first baby in the family in 7 years. Addison hasn't quite got use to being pregnant. She worries if she is going to stop working.

"This is a time to be joyful. Work will always be there." Christina is more excited for Addison than she is. The idea of a beautiful new baby is amazing. Addison is a bit nervous because she hasn't been a new mother in 13 years. She had a nanny for her other two children. Gradually, she's getting excited. It's official. She's excited. She's shopping for the new baby.

They go to a doctor's visit for the ultrasound. They find out that she has not one but two babies inside her. They are having boys. Everything is falling into place. Kenny is beside himself with joy. He can't wait to have little clones of himself. This is wonderful holiday news.

Patrick finds out that Addison is pregnant. He starts telling mutual associates that she is having his baby. She confronts him.

"I never told anyone that. When they told me you were pregnant, they assumed it was my baby. I didn't correct them because I wished it were my baby."

"You are fucking crazy. I have begged you to stay out of my life. What the fuck does it take to get rid of you?"

"Let me lick your asshole. I want to fuck you like I did when we were younger. You just need me to take your virginity again. Then, you will love and want to marry me. Don't let my ex wife come in between what we have. Yes, I was married but I was unhappy. Why can't you understand that?"

"Leave me and my family alone." Addison hangs up the phone.

He begins calling her employer. He is asking for her work schedule. They refuse. The employer quickly informs Addison. When Addison speaks with him, she is calm. She asked him to please stop calling her job. Patrick tells her that he needs another job to help support his kids.

"You mean your college professor job isn't taking care of them?"

"No, I don't make that much there. I need you to get me on with your company or at least give me a reference letter."

"Ok, wait on it."

Patrick applies for a job with Addison's company. He sends his resume to Addison's assistant. He has a resume that is full of lies. On the resume, he says that he is a ramp supervisor. He's not. For entertainment purposes, Addison has her assistant call Patrick's employment for verification. They tell her that Patrick is no supervisor. She asked a few more questions pertaining to his resume. His supervisor is surprised that Patrick lied on his resume. The assistant kindly tells the supervisor, thank you. She tells him to inform Patrick that his resume and application has been thrown out due to falsification.

Patrick has one of his co-workers call Addison pretending that he is the appropriate supervisor.

"Hello, may I speak to Ms. Addison?"

"This is she, who is this?"

"My name is Mr. Smith, I understand that called earlier and had some questions pertaining to Patrick. I am the person that you need to speak with."

"Really, because the supervisor that my assistant spoke to seem to have the answers we needed."

"Well, he doesn't know exactly what Patrick does. I am happy to answer any questions that you may have."

"I'm not sure how your company works. This is very unprofessional."

"Why are you getting so worked up?"

"You called me. I do not appreciate playing games. Please don't make me call your employer and have you two terminated."

"I apologize for upsetting you Ms. Addison. No, it will not be necessary for you to contact our employer. Good Bye."

Addison and Christina have come to find out that Patrick manipulates people into lying for him. Addison tells Christina that the only reason she is not contacting his employer is because of the children. Without that piece of job, they wouldn't get child support.

Patrick figures he has to gain something from this entire Addison fiasco. Patrick is traveling on her company's airline. He is running late to the airport. When he gets there, they do not allow him to board because he is too late. He causes a scene. He's yelling, "Who is your boss? I demand to see Addison. She will have you fired." He's going on and on. He makes such a spectacle that the airline documents the situation. In the notes, they band Patrick from traveling privileges on the airline. It's one thing after another with Patrick. She is so frustrated. "Is he trying to get me fired?" Christina doesn't know what to tell her.

He is unpredictable because the entire situation has been out of his control for so long. He never says anything to Addison of this incidence. She was informed by her employer.

CHAPTER 28

PITTS SKY BOX, CALLING HER FAMILY (LADY CALLS ADDISON ABOUT BEING PREGNANT)

Patrick doesn't believe that Addison is sharing any of these experiences with her family. He thinks that she is keeping them to herself. In his mind she is coming back to him eventually. The process is taking longer than he wants. Addison is telling her dad, mom, sisters, Mario and her brothers. Her brother is fed up with Patrick.

Patrick is calling Addison's family. First, he calls her grandparents. He is calling to tell them how much he loves their granddaughter. He wants to know if he can come visit them in Pittsburg. "Baby, my granddaughter is married. That wouldn't be respectful to her husband." He strikes out there.

Second, he calls her mom. He tells her that he loves Addison. He asked her if she can talk to her. He wants her to give Addison the green light on dating him.

"If she doesn't want to talk to you, I can't make her. I don't agree with a married man dating my daughter anyway. That's not acceptable to me or my family. If she's not talking to you maybe it's for the best."

"Yes mam, I understand but I am not married anymore. I was unhappy. Addison is the love of my life. I want a chance at happiness with her. I know how much she values your input. If you can just help me out, I promise I will make her happy." "I can't help you." They hang up the phone.

Third, he calls her father. Her father can't believe that Patrick is calling him. He wanted to hear what he had to say.

"Hi, Mr. Addison, this is Patrick."

"Hello."

"I am calling you to apologize for any hurt I have caused your daughter in the past. I was young and dumb then. I would like the opportunity to be a better man to her. I have always viewed you as a father to me. I think of your family as a second family. I am hoping that I can join you for this Thanksgiving. I have no where else to go. There is no better place I'd rather be than with my family (you all). May I have to pleasure of joining your family for the holidays?"

"What about your own family? I understand that you have a wife and three kids. I do not approve of a man who walks out on his wife and children. This is exactly what you have done. Now, you want me to give you permission to be with my daughter. What makes you think this is ok? Don't you think you should at least be with your kids for the holidays?"

"Yes sir, my ex wife is not allowing me to see them. She is a very petty and bitter woman. I don't want the kids to see us argue. I have not walked out on my kids. I send them $1000 each per month in child support. I just want to be happy. In all my life, the only times I were truly happy is when I was with your daughter. I have no mother. She was killed. When she was living, she didn't take care of me. She was an alcoholic. Don't I deserve some happiness?"

"Everyone deserves some happiness son. What do you think will make you happy other than my daughter?"

"I don't know Sir. I know that I want to marry her and have children with her. We should have been together all along."

"My daughter is happily married with children. She has told you that on several occasions. Yes, she and her husband have their issues but they are a family. She turned to you when she thought she was getting a divorce. All you did was deceive her. What were you planning? Whatever it is I am glad that she found you out sooner than later. You need to do some soul searching. You need to get your life together. After this call, you can't call me to talk about my daughter anymore. You can call and say that you've got your life together. Otherwise, I will not help you destroy my daughter's life. Have a good life Patrick."

Patrick is crying like a baby on the phone. Mr. Addison feels somewhat sorry for Patrick, however, not too sorry. Addison has told her father a lot of what Patrick has done. He just couldn't believe that he called him.

A couple of weeks go by. Patrick tells his friends Gusto and Arny that Addison's dad has a Pittsburg Steelers sky box. He's already made contact with him and they are good to go. They plan a road trip. They think that Patrick has connections like when they went to Mario's VIP room. They get to the stadium. Patrick looks up her father's sky box. He rings for someone to let him in. Addison's brother is there. He has been fed up with Patrick and is ready to whip his ass.

He goes to the entry. Patrick and his boys are standing there waiting to enter. He asked Patrick what he wants.

"You have no place here. What in the hell are you doing here?"

"I just came by to see Mr. Addison. What's the problem man?"

"You're the problem. Nobody here wants to see you."

"Hey man, I know that you are angry with me for not telling your sister that I was married. We are working through that."

"Stop lying mother fucker."

By now, Gusto and Arny walk away giving Patrick some privacy.

"My sister has a husband. They are about to have a baby. It is not your baby. Stop fucking stalking her."

"I love her, I'm not stalking her."

Mr. Addison has come down. "Is there a problem?"

"No Sir, no problem. I was just stopping in to say hello."

Her brother wants to fight Patrick. He and Kenny are really close brothers. They return to the sky box and enjoy the rest of the game. Of course, her brother calls her to give her all of the details. She calls Christina because every time they think Patrick can't do anything crazier, he proves them wrong.

Patrick tells Gusto and Arny that Addison's brother is angry with him. He is angry because he hurt his sister. He says that he is playing the protective big brother role. He tells them that he has to give it time. Once Addison forgives him for being married then all will be fine again. The guys say okay. They go and watch the game like the commoners.

Patrick calls Addison.

"You have your entire family hating me. Why did you have to tell them our business? I guess you got what you want. Your brother wants to fight me. I will not fight him out of respect for you. You need to tell him to stay the hell out of my face."

"Get a fucking life."

Addison hangs up the phone. Patrick calls her fifty more times that day. Addison has been trying to keep Kenny from finding out that Patrick won't leave her alone. He knows she and Kenny are having a baby. They are moving on. She doesn't want to cause any drama between her and Kenny. The only person she feels that she can talk to that can understand is Christina. The truth is Christina is the only one that understands how crazy Patrick is. Christina is happy he has got the hell away from her and the children.

Patrick has been calling Addison relentlessly. He has been calling her sister asking if he can talk to her. She thinks it's just crazy, lying Patrick. Soon after all of this madness, Addison gets a phone call. It is a woman. This woman asked to speak with her. The woman tells Addison that she is pregnant with Patrick's baby. She wants to know what's so special about her.

"I want you to leave him alone. I checked his phone records and your number is in here too many times to count. I want you to not take anymore of his calls. You are going to cause him not to have contact with our baby."

"First of all, who is this?"

"Don't worry about that-the only thing you need to know is that Patrick is with me."

"Ok, you called my phone. I didn't give you my number. How did you get it? You need to get your facts straight sweetheart. Patrick had a wife and three kids. I'm not the reason that he doesn't want to be with you. They are. He doesn't want that to get back to his ex wife. You're calling the wrong woman"

"No, he told me that he made a bad judgment in leaving her for you. You destroyed his life with your games. I got your number out of his phone. Leave him alone."

"If you got my number out of his phone, you should be telling him to leave me alone. I have not called him once. Check the call history."

Patrick calls Addison's sister. He asked to speak with Addison. She lets Patrick hear the drama that he has created. Addison and her sister put the two of them on speaker phone. Patrick is yelling through the phone. He's telling the pregnant woman to leave Addison alone.

"This is between you and me. Don't call her anymore."

"You need to tell this bitch that we are together." Eventually, Addison and her sister hang up on both of their stupid asses. Unbelievable. Christina and Addison try to figure out if that was a staged performance or if it is true.

Patrick calls Addison back crying. He is saying that he has completely screwed up his life. He's telling her that Christina was a good wife. He did some things that he is not proud of. He just needs her to be his friend.

"I can't be that person for you any more, Patrick. Too much has happened."

His boyfriend Arny tells a mutual friend that Patrick has a new baby on the way. It gets back to Addison. They conclude that it is true. "How in the hell can he afford another child? He's not paying for the ones he have. He's a loser."

CHAPTER 29

PATRICK EXPLODES ON ADDISON

Addison finally experiences the Patrick that Christina has been dealing with for the last year. Patrick has had it with Addison. He is being constantly questioned by his sisters. They want to know the status of him and Addison's relationship. They want him to start bringing her around. He feels that he looks foolish. He had told them that he can't wait to divorce Christina. It appears to them that he has lost Christina and his children. It doesn't look like he and Addison are together.

He finally tells them that he and Addison have broken up. He says that she couldn't get pass the marriage thing. Patrick begins parading some old girlfriend around his family. He doesn't have the connection to this person as with Addison. She doesn't have any money to support him. He doesn't have any money to even take her out. This relationship doesn't last long.

One night, Patrick is sitting around lonely. He is thinking of all that he has lost. He becomes angry. Addison was his parachute. She was supposed to pick up taking care of him where Christina left off. She would have given him the legitimacy he needed to continue being scandalous. He doesn't know where to turn. He calls Addison.

"I need a few minutes of your time."

"What now Patrick. What is it this time? You have three minutes."

"I have done nothing but prove my love to you. I gave up my family to be with you. What makes you think that you are so much better than me? You are nothing to me anymore. I can't believe that you went back to your so called husband. And you are having a baby with that mother fucker. I hate you and hope your baby dies."

Addison hangs up the phone. She can't believe that Patrick told her that he hopes her baby dies. She thinks that it's a little funny. She doesn't care what he says but it stings. She calls Christina. Christina tells her that she is so sorry that she had to experience that asshole. Christina refuses to repeat what Patrick said to her. She believes that the more you say something the better chances of it happening. They agree that he is a nothing ass guy. They move on to talking about something else. For the first time in this entire process, Addison is able to empathize with the experiences Christina has had with Patrick.

At this point, one would expect Patrick to never contact Addison again. This loser calls her the next day. On her voicemail, he apologizes for his outbursts the day before. He says that he was going through something. He shouldn't have taken it out on her.

He has no conscience. It doesn't matter who he hurts. The only time he shows any remorse is when he is caught. It's not remorse because he hurt anyone. It's remorse because he is busted. He expects people to forget and move on in the same direction before the trust was broken.

CHAPTER 30

ADDISON'S BABIES PASS AWAY

It has been weeks since Christina has heard from Addison. She calls to check in on her. She wants to know how she is doing. She asked her how the pregnancy was going. Addison informs her that she had a little scare. She started cramping and clotting really bad. She went to the hospital and had to stay for three days. However, everything is fine. She is put on bed rest for the remainder of the pregnancy. Her mother came to town to take care of her.

They discuss Addison leaving her career all together. She wants her company to allow her to work from home after the babies are born. She wants to negotiate some light duties. If they do not agree with her proposal then they will have to part ways. Her company merged with another major company. If she plans on continuing employment with them after the pregnancy, she will have to relocate to Atlanta, Georgia.

Kenny is fine with that. His job is based in Atlanta, GA. He commutes back and forth to Minnesota. Addison is not sure if she wants to take the kids out of their comfort zones. She does want to get out of the cold. However, the thought of being pregnant, relocating and taking a new job in another state is all too overwhelming.

A few weeks pass. Addison begins having strong contractions again. She is rushed to the hospital. She is about to deliver the twins prematurely. They are born without all of their organs. One baby dies immediately. The other is alive for nearly two weeks. She calls Christina from the hospital. Christina asked if everything was okay. At first Addison is talking normal. She begins to cry.

"What's the matter? OMG."

"I am in the hospital. The babies arrived early. My first son has died. The other is in intensive care." Christina cries for Addison and her family.

"I am so sorry."

"I have been here for six days. I need to get out of here. It is so depressing. I am in the ward with women who have all lost babies. I have to go now; my mom needs me to let her back into the area."

"Ok, if there is anything that I can do, please call me. I will be praying for you and the family."

Christina can't help but to remember what Patrick said to her a few weeks earlier. She feels really sad for Addison. She was looking forward to becoming a new mommy again. She was looking forward to the new beginnings that they would bring for her entire family.

Soon after, they plan a funeral for the two baby boys. Christina calls Addison every other day to check in. Addison's family is there for her. Her mother stays for a few months. Addison's brother is helping Kenny through. The girls are worried about their mother.

Christina works from home. Addison's work schedule has always been quite flexible. They talk often. They talk about everything and anything to help Addison through the day. They discuss Christina's dating life. This is an interesting topic. Christina tells her of a guy that she met on a chat line. The guy is in town for a construction project.

The man is 8 years younger than her. She is teased for being a cougar. He is the best sex that she has had in her life. Addison calls Christina when she is having a meltdown. Christina listens. She doesn't know anything else to do. She doesn't know what to say. She just listens until the conversation changes directions.

CHAPTER 31

CHILD SUPPORT ISSUES, CALLS TO CHILDREN, LAST VISIT TELLING THEM HE WAS HOMELESS

Patrick is living in Detroit, MI. He had not paid child support since leaving. He calls Christina to tell her that he is getting unemployment. He says that he was laid off. He asked her if he can begin communicating with the children again. She tells him yes but it must be after after 9pm when her cell phone is free. Christina is receiving eighty-two dollars per week for three children. She is not impressed to say the least. She has to laugh from time to time. She calls Samone to tell her that the eighty-two dollars is more than she was getting from him when they were married. They both laugh. It helps put things in perspective.

Patrick begins calling the children at nine p.m. He would ask about their day. He would question them about their school work. When he would ask them a question, they answer yes. He would have the nerve to correct them with telling them to say yes sir. The more he spoke with them the more it made Christina angry. She's thinking, here she is busting her ass to raise three children alone and this ass hole calls expecting respect and acknowledgement. He urks the hell out of her.

The kids are pretty happy to speak with him. Christina feels that it is better if the kids love Patrick from a distance. It's not important for them to talk to him everyday. He isn't doing a damn thing. He wants to keep their minds on him. As she listens to their conversations with him, she flips out.

"Who in the hell do you think you are? You are insignificant. I will not teach them that it's ok for a father to abandon his children. When I stopped providing for you, you stopped doing anything for them. You are so insignificant. Do not question them. They don't need a grown ass friend. Get your own life, leave us the fuck alone."

"I do take care of them. They are my children and I can ask them whatever I want. So what you are doing everything. That has nothing to do with me being their father. I get to make decisions about what they do. I am their father and you hate that they love me"

"Like hell you make decisions regarding them. No, I hate that you are a manipulative bastard. You don't deserve their love. You act like you are doing something. You aren't doing shit. Truth be told you don't even deserve their respect."

She hangs up the phone. He attempts calling back but no answer. Christina allows the children to talk to Patrick once or twice a week. Many times Patrick call the kids don't even want to talk to him. Christina asked them why. They say that they don't have anything to talk about.

Patrick calls Christina and questions her about talking to the children every night. Christina politely tells him that the kids talking to him is not a priority. Her priorities are raising her children.

"I give less than a damn if they ever speak to or see you again. However, they are often busy. They have places to be, people to see, and things to do. When they are available I will give them the phone and allow them to talk. I will not explain myself to you again."

The last time Patrick visited the children, he told them that he has been homeless. He said that their mommy gets mad at him because he has no money to help with them. The kids cry. They feel sorry for their dad. Who does that to their children? Why would he tell them that?

Christina debriefs her children when Patrick drops them off. She gets pissed off when they talk about their dad being homeless. It's really hard for her to keep her cool.

"He wasn't homeless when we had to move from our old home because he wouldn't leave. He no longer lives there because he wasn't paying any bills. He was stealing the mortgage from us. If mommy hadn't moved us we'd be homeless."

The kids don't like to hear anything bad about their dad. Christina finds herself always trying to set the record straight after they have talked to Patrick. He always makes himself look like the victim. It is sickening. She wants him to take some damn responsibilities for his actions. He needs to stop blaming everyone else for his current situation.

Christina has learned that talking to Patrick is such a waste of time. She chooses not to engage because she knows every word out of his mouth is a lie. She feels that he always has an agenda. He doesn't act like a normal and rational person. He lies to himself and others. She has learned to deal with only the facts with Patrick. Those facts have to be tangible. Otherwise, Patrick tries to manipulate anything. Lying is as natural to him as breathing. Now, that's the sad truth.

CHAPTER 32

GUSTO CALLS CHRISTINA 1 YEAR AFTER THE DIVORCE

Christina gets an email from Gusto requesting that she call him. Gusto and Patrick grew up together. He was the best man in their wedding. Christina hasn't communicated with anyone that she met through Patrick. However, Christina and Gusto went to undergrad together, therefore, they had a relationship without Patrick. Gusto didn't have Christina's number but he found her on their Alumni website. Christina calls Gusto and they begin to talk.

Gusto begins with apologizing for not reaching out to Christina and the kids prior to now. He asked how they were doing. Christina responds with all is great on our end. She tells Gusto that she didn't expect to hear from him. She understands that he is Patrick's friend. She understands that Patrick has his support system and she has hers. Christina goes on to say to Gusto that she knows that he didn't call to play catch up. She directly asked him what he wants.

Gusto begins his story with "I am afraid for Patrick." He says that Patrick is doing some really bad things. He tells her that it seems as if he has some sort of chemical dependency. He says that he wanted some insight on what she may have experienced with Patrick that caused their divorce. He said that it's always two sides to every story. He expresses that the things Patrick were saying that she did just didn't sound like her. He says that he listened. He didn't believe that she could have been so cold and unreasonable. He was told that she was a calculating, cheating, lying, thieving bitch.

Christina has an interesting personality. She didn't really care what Patrick had told anyone. She expressed to Gusto that she expected him to contact her. She had found out that Patrick was working for his property management company several months earlier. She tells Gusto that she had hoped that he didn't have Patrick handling any money or paperwork. Gusto interjects and says he wished he would've known sooner than later.

Christina tells Gusto that she will share the experiences that led her to get away from Patrick. She would explain why she needed to divorce him. She tells him that after she shares then he would need to share as well. He agreed.

She begins with telling Gusto that Patrick was stealing the mortgage checks. She tells him that she had caught Patrick having an affair a few months prior to the mortgage discovery. She explains to Gusto that she had no trust in Patrick.

She explains that they were in bankruptcy. They had to pay eight hundred and fifty dollars bi-weekly. She tells Gusto that Patrick was supposed to be working a delivery job from midnight until 4 a.m. She tells him that she found out instead of Patrick working each night; he would be at Nina's apartment fucking.

Instead of both of them paying the mortgage, she was paying it alone. Gusto is listening intensely. Gusto tells Christina that he had no knowledge of any affair or stolen mortgage. She says of course you wouldn't know. After all, why would Patrick tell you something that might suggests that he is the actual liar, cheat and thief?

She tells him that they had cashier checks made out to the bankruptcy trustee. Patrick was going to the credit union cancelling the checks made out to the trustee. He would cash them out and spend the money on whatever his dependency. He would then bring her the receipts saying that he had mailed the mortgage.

When she got the semi- annual statement in the mail. She immediately noticed that there were several payments missing. She proceeds with the rest of that story. She explains that Patrick lied the entire process and only admitted the truth after the bank accountant provided the proof of his signatures.

She tells him that she began to find out one thing after another from there. She was so terrified of Patrick. She felt he was a complete stranger. She explains that she would sleep with her door locked and purse under her pillow. She tells Gusto that she couldn't get past the calculation of stealing the cashier checks, denying it and then trying to blame it on her. She feels that Patrick is capable of anything. If someone tells her that Patrick is a Pedi filer she would believe him. She explains that because Patrick is such a con artist, she doesn't trust the children to be in Michigan with him.

She thinks that the bad things that he does may cause harm to the children. She hasn't felt comfortable with him alone with the children. She feels that Patrick lies about everything; therefore it is a total waste of time to talk to him. She chooses to deal with him only when necessary.

Christina tells Gusto that she doesn't know what a person act or look like when they are on drugs. Therefore, she doesn't know what drug Patrick is using. She never found out what he did with the eleven thousand dollars he had stolen. She tells Gusto that she didn't notice new things or anything. Patrick told Christina that he was gambling and he lost it all.

Gusto says that he has known Patrick since they were kids. He has never known him to gamble. He begins to share his recent experiences with Christina. He begins with the fact that Patrick was managing an apartment building for his company. Patrick's responsibilities included collecting the rent from tenants. The tenants were told to write checks in his company's name. Patrick would get a 50% commission on all new tenants. Also, he got a free apartment with the job. The only thing he was required to pay was $30 for utilities.

Gusto tells Christina that he was sending money to Ohio to help Patrick after they split. He says that he felt sorry for Patrick and the entire situation that he was experiencing with her. Patrick said that he was not allowed to see his kids because Christina was bitter. He told Gusto that he didn't have any money because the court awarded that he pay all of his money in alimony and child support.

The down fall of their business relationship started with one future tenant. There was a male tenant that Gusto had solicited to move into the apartment building. He gave Patrick all of the information and asked him to follow up. One month goes by and no tenant. Two months goes by and the tenant has not moved in. When Gusto asked Patrick about the tenant, Patrick tells him that the guy chose to wait. Gusto decides to call the guy himself. Gusto asked the guy what's the problem. What can I do to get you moved into my property? The guy says, what are you talking about I have been here for the last two months.

Gusto is in complete shock. He calls Patrick and asked him to explain why the tenant says he has been living there for months now. Patrick got really defensive screaming "he doesn't live here, he is lying." Gusto asked Patrick why he would be lying. Patrick says that he doesn't know. Gusto tells Patrick to explain why the tenant has receipts. Patrick says that the guy needed receipts before he could move in for some kind of hustle that he was running.

Gusto goes into the office with Patrick. He calls the guy on speaker phone. Gusto wanted Patrick to hear what the guy was saying. The guy tells Gusto to come to the apartment where he has been living for the last two months. It was then that Patrick concedes by telling Gusto that the guy is telling the truth.

Gusto gets off the phone with the tenant. He is in absolute shock. He wants to know why Patrick has stolen the money and lied about it. He wants to know what Patrick is thinking. Patrick tells him that he has a gambling problem.

He cries and cries like a baby. He tells Gusto that Christina has taken all of his money. He says that he has nothing. He explains that he is desperate. He says that he is really messed up after the divorce experience. He tells him that he is doing crazy things because Christina has taken the children away from him.

Gusto feels sorry for poor old Patrick. He tells Patrick that he has got to get it together. He says that a man might kill him if he steals his money. He goes on to say that he loves him and wants to see him do better for himself. He says that he would help him out this one time. He explained to Patrick that he understands the pain he is feeling. He asked Patrick if there is anything else that he should know. Patrick says no and swears that he only stole the rent 2 times.

Gusto soon learned that Patrick had more lies that he didn't share. One day the owner of the property calls Gusto. He says that he has 4 or 5 tenants that have always paid their rent on time. He continues to say that since Patrick has been property manager each of them are 2 months behind. He wanted Gusto to explain. He tells Gusto that there is something shady going on with his employee. Gusto argued with the owner stating that he has known Patrick for thirty years. He says that he trusts Patrick. He tells the owner that he doesn't know why the tenants have not paid.

The owner calls the tenants to ask why they haven't paid rent in two months. Each of the tenants says that they had paid. They tell him that they have receipts. The property owner goes to the apartment building and fires Patrick. The property owner calls Gusto. He tells him that he has fired Patrick. He explains that Patrick has been stealing the rent money. He says that he no longer requires the services of his property management company.

This contract was a third of Gusto Company's income. That was a huge financial loss. The property owner goes on to say that he is going to prosecute Patrick. Gusto is outdone. He can't believe that Patrick would screw over him like this. Especially, after he has helped him so much. Gusto begins to suspect that Patrick is on some kind of drug.

Gusto tells the property owner that he is going to take responsibility. He says that Patrick worked for his company so he is responsible. He asked the owner not to prosecute Patrick. They set up a payment plan. Gusto was going to pay $250 per month until the $4000 is paid back in full. The owner tells Gusto that he shouldn't be taking the fall for Patrick. He said that Patrick needs to have consequences for his actions.

Gusto goes over to see Patrick at his apartment. He asked Patrick about the other tenants' rent. Patrick said that they hadn't paid any rent. He goes into a roar about people always lying on him. He swears to God to Gusto that they didn't pay. Gusto tells Patrick that they all had receipts. He asked Patrick why he is doing this.

Patrick breaks down and begins to cry like a baby again. Patrick is crying because he is caught. But Gusto doesn't know this. All Gusto knows is that he sees his friend crying like a baby. He knows that Patrick has a problem. He feels that someone is going to hurt Patrick. He has known Patrick all of their childhood. He has brotherly love for Patrick. They grew up as best friends. They were the best man for each others wedding.

Gusto decides to tell Patrick that he is there for him. He feels that Patrick is at his lowest point. Patrick sees that he has Gusto exactly where he wants him. Gusto is feeling sorry for Patrick. Patrick decides to tell Gusto that it is his two son's birthday. He says that he has never missed a birthday. He says that he just wanted to see them but he has no money.

Because of the love Gusto has for Patrick, he reached into his pocket and gave Patrick $150. He tells him to go see his children and buy them something for their birthday. Patrick has no remorse. He takes the money as if he is getting a loan. He acts like Gusto has totally forgotten about him stealing the rent money. Gusto departs hoping that Patrick would get himself together. Gusto is simply overwhelmed with this entire experience.

One month goes by and Gusto has paid his first restitution payment. At this point, Gusto got a call from a guy who had given Patrick a deposit to move into the apartment building. Gusto finds out that Patrick is still operating under the assumption that he is working under his property management company. Gusto tells the man that Patrick no longer works for his company. He apologizes to the man. He says that he would contact Patrick. He agrees to help set up a payment plan where the man can get his $750 back.

Gusto contacts Patrick and tells him that this man has contacted him about a deposit he paid him. He told Patrick that he is going to have to handle this himself. He told Patrick that he is done bailing him out. He puts the two in contact with one another. Gusto tells the man that if ever he can't get in touch with Patrick, he is welcome to call him. Gusto is acting as a mediator between the two. Gusto feels that it is the least he can do to assist in getting the man his money back. After all, Patrick was using his property management name.

Patrick pays the man the first payment of $125. Each scheduled pay date, the man calls Patrick. Each time after that Patrick says that he is on his way and never shows up to pay. By this time, the man is clearly frustrated and angry. He calls Gusto and tells him the experiences he is having with Patrick. He tells Gusto that he and his cousin are about ready to take it to the streets. Gusto tells the man to let him try contacting Patrick. Patrick decides that he is no longer going to answer calls from either of them.

By now Gusto has made his second payment of $250. After counsel from his wife, Gusto has decided that he can no longer pay the restitution. Gusto's wife tells him that Patrick needs consequences for his actions. She tells him that he is enabling Patrick's behavior. He tells the apartment owner that he needs to do what has to be done. He explains that he simply can't afford it. He had been laid off from his job for the last two months. He apologizes for the bad business.

During the time Patrick was working for Gusto, he found a 2 family flat to manage. This was before Gusto had discovered Patrick stealing. Gusto tells Patrick to manage that himself. He says that Patrick could have all of the profits. He didn't have to document that property under the company.

Patrick decides that he and Arny can rent the place. Arny has given Patrick his portion of the rent for the last two months. Patrick gets cable for the two of them. He put it in the man's name that he owed the deposit money. Gusto finds out that Patrick has stolen this man's identity. Patrick had not paid the owner of the property one cent. She is in the process of having them evicted.

In the meanwhile, Arny calls Gusto. He asked Gusto if he knows what is going on with Patrick. He said that someone had put some fake drugs on their porch. Arny wanted to know what transpired between the two of them. Gusto told Arny that he is going to call Christina. By now he has figured that Patrick was doing the same type of stuff in Ohio. He thought that it must be the reason for the divorce. He figures that Christina can give him an idea of what he is dealing with Patrick.

At this point, both Gusto and Arny feel the need to distance them selves from Patrick. They feel that Patrick is putting them in harms way by lying, stealing, and cheating people.

Christina tells Gusto that Patrick is going to get exactly what he deserves. She explained that she was not being mean. She tells him that when you plant weeds they eventually grow up. She says that they either kill the good grass or have to be destroyed. This is what has happened to Patrick. His weeds have grown up. They are killing everything good around them. Once they destroy all the good grasses, then eventually the weeds have to die. Usually, the weeds aren't killed until they have done irreparable damage. In other words, you reap what you sew.

Christina explains to Gusto that yes she believes that Patrick is on some sort of drug. She goes on to say that she believes that Patrick has some sort of mental imbalance. She points to examples that both she and Gusto had experienced with Patrick. She explains that these are all reasons the children can never come to be with him in Detroit. She says that she would never knowingly put them in harms way, not even for a weekend break.

She tells Gusto that she believes that Patrick has always been manipulative and conning. She doesn't believe that he has ever had to take responsibility for his actions. For example, Gusto gave Patrick $150 even after he knew about the stolen rent. It seems that Patrick somehow always becomes the victim. People feel sorry for him because of his soft and humble demeanor. Patrick needs professional help. The help that he needs is beyond their scope. Christina had to let Patrick go because she couldn't afford to be destroyed by him.

Christina tells Gusto that whatever drug Patrick is using, he has been using since before she married him. She reminds him of a conversation the two of them had the first month they were married. Gusto had called Patrick with concern. He had been told by a very reliable source that Patrick was on drugs. Patrick got so angry that Christina overheard him cursing during the conversation with Gusto. She asked Patrick what was the matter? Patrick had told her that someone was spreading a rumor that he was on drugs. Christina didn't think much about it afterwards. Gusto remembered how angry Patrick got and he threatened to kill the person that told Gusto. Gusto explained to Patrick that he was just calling to let him know that no matter what he was there for him.

Christina tells Gusto that she believes that Patrick was running when he moved to Chicago with her. She believes that he owed someone some money. She says that Patrick was drinking one night with her brother in law. He told him that his mother was killed because he owed someone money. Of course, Patrick denies saying that. Why would Steve lie on Patrick? Money has always come up missing but Christina chalked it up as learning to be married and joint account trials and errors. She believes that Patrick has always stolen money to support his habit.

Christina tells Gusto that the reason Patrick burned them is because they gave him access. He had access to their money. Gusto wants to know what Patrick believed would happen once they found him out. She tells him that she doesn't believe that he plans it out that way. She believes that his plan goes as far as getting what he wants for the moment. After Patrick does his dirty deeds, he dismisses them as if they never happened. It's like he convinces himself and that's why he is so good at convincing others. He can be so adamant about his lie.

After the fake drug incident, Patrick leaves town. He decides to go to the country in Alabama to visit his dad. Basically, he is running again. He thinks that if he disappears for awhile then people would forget. He'll forget.

She tells Gusto that she predicts Patrick to live off his father until he passes away. She says that it would be just. She believes that his dad raised him to be the man he has become. She explains that all of your son's using drugs is not normal. One son and wife being killed is not normal. Based on her experiences with Patrick's father, he too is always the victim. He never takes responsibility for his role in any situation.

Gusto tells Christina that he hopes Patrick hits rock bottom and gets help. He doesn't want anyone to kill Patrick. Christina tells him that she feels the same way. She wouldn't want her kids to have to suffer that pain. They say good bye and I love you. Gusto agrees to keep in touch with Christina.

After Christina gets off the phone, she is just blown away. The first person she calls is Addison, secondly, her brother, thirdly, Samone, fourthly and fifthly her sisters. She and Addison thank God one more time for trusting each other. They agree that it was a smart decision not to let Patrick no anything about their maneuvers. Her brother says, wow, he is going back to people he has known and burning bridges. Samone says just when you think it can't get any crazier; Patrick gives us one more surprise after the other. Both her sisters say that someone is going to hurt him.

The funny thing is that Patrick has been calling for the children every other day. He has been acting as if he is legitimately getting his life in order. He has been acting as if everything is all wonderful. But Christina realizes that in Patrick's mind all is good. He has forgotten about all of the damage he has caused.

Christina is so grateful that she was able to see Patrick through Addison's eyes when they were co existing. Because, until you really know that Patrick is a fraud, you wouldn't believe it.

CHAPTER 33

PATRICK REVEALED

Patrick has established himself as a person not to be trusted. Many of his love ones have distanced themselves from him. Others that don't know him well think that he is weird. Patrick doesn't see himself the way others do. He is totally oblivious to people's reactions to him. He thinks that he is indeed a sly fox. The problem is that Patrick forgets the lies he tells. He expects others to do the same. Therefore, when Patrick reappears on the scene people are suspicious of him.

His sisters allow him to sleep over their house for a couple of days at a time. They pay for his cell phone so that he can look for a job and communicate with his children. They feed him. They don't have any money to give him. They feel sorry for him. They wish that Christina had never found anything out. At least, he would have a warm bed every night. Patrick hasn't been able to find a steady relationship because women need a man that can help provide. Once they realize Patrick is not the man he says he is they leave him alone.

His children love him. They remember Patrick when he was married to their mom. They remember the happy family they had before he was found out. They talk with him once a week or so. They are healthy beautiful children. The youngest don't really know him. However, he does know that Patrick is his dad.

Christina is happy with the kids loving Patrick from a far. She doesn't want Patrick to teach their children to be anything like him. The only way to assure that is for him to stay away. The truth is he can't help manipulating and hurting people, especially, those that love him.

Patrick's sisters are telling him to move back to Ohio to be around his children. They are trying to get him out of Detroit.

They are tired of taking care of him. He returns to Ohio to harass Christina for a period of time. There is no one in Ohio that will take care of Patrick. He doesn't stay there long.

Patrick's sisters convince him to move to Alabama. They are afraid that he will meet the same fate of their oldest brother. He was killed in Detroit. They never found the killer. His brother was doing the same things that Patrick is doing. They gathered up enough money to get him there. They hold a family meeting. They cook him dinner and express how much they love him.

Eventually, Patrick moves to the country in Alabama with his dad. They live in a trailer. There is really no where to work within a 30 mile radius. Patrick works for his uncle cutting grass. He hunts and fish for his food. His dad has a garden for their vegetables. The money he makes from his uncle, he uses to buy drugs. He bombs cigarettes and beer off his dad. His dad gets tired of taking care of him. However, one thing is clear, he's happy that he is alive. Patrick floats back and forth between Alabama, Detroit and Ohio.

CHAPTER 34

ALL PARTIES MOVE FORWARD — BETTER, WISER, STRONGER, FAITHFUL AND GRATEFUL

Addison and her family work on healing after the loss of the twins. They choose to relocate to Atlanta for a fresh start. They all transition quite well. The girls love their new schools. They love the programs they are participating in. Addison has smoothly moved into her new position in her company. She is enjoying hanging out with old college friends. Her parents are there visiting more often than not.

She doesn't talk to Patrick at all. She and Christina keep in touch mostly via face book. However, whenever Christina is in Atlanta they get together for dinner and drinks. The only thing they discuss about Patrick is being grateful to each other.

She and Kenny are doing great. She feels that is thanks to the Patrick experience. They are healing and happy together. They have a greater appreciation for each other and the family.

Christina and the children have a great support system. They continue to prosper. The kids are getting better and better in sports. They help their mother out tremendously. They are becoming more independent. They don't talk much about their dad or wonder what he's doing. When they talk to him, they are respectful. They are happy to talk to him.

Christina has adjusted quite well to being a single mother. She has even learned how to take care of her needs and wants first. She has started back playing volleyball and softball two or three times a week. She has no regrets. She is grateful everyday for the wisdom from this experience. Regardless to how the marriage ended she is grateful for the times that were good.

She continues to limit communication between herself and Patrick. She knows he is a compulsive liar. She has no desire to ever engage in dialogue with him. She is not bitter. She just thinks that it takes too much negative energy. She continues to monitor the kids dialog with him simply to protect them. She doesn't always say anything only when she feels it is necessary. She is so grateful that he lives so many miles away. She feels the farther away he is the less damage he can do.

CHAPTER 35

PATRICK'S CHARACTER

Patrick is a fox in sheep's clothing. All of his life he has blamed others for his current circumstances. He appears to be kind, humble and nice. People meet him and think hey, now that's a nice guy. This is his outer shell. He is the youngest of 6 children. His closest sibling is 10 years older than him. He has 3 sisters and 2 brothers. His parents are the age of most grandparents. His mom and dad are from the south. They like many others migrated to the north for factory jobs. His parents were both alcoholics. His brothers and male cousins drug addicts. His father and uncles all male chauvinists.

Patrick possesses all of these traits and more. However, the distinct difference is that the other males in Patrick's life show their personalities quite well. Patrick on the other hand appears to be a kind and gentle soul. Patrick was raised mostly by his sisters, the streets, alcoholic parents and men that had no respect for the women in their lives. The saying that the apple doesn't fall far from the tree is certainly true for Patrick. Because of this dysfunctional background, Patrick chose to learn to be pretty crafty. He had to learn to adapt to whichever environment he found himself in. Survival of the fittest would be a phrase to describe his adaptations.

Patrick's character is one of a quiet nature. A good friend that listens to you. He doesn't give up much information on himself but he listens with a purpose. A person that you wouldn't want anyone to take advantage of. A person that you might feel the need to protect because he doesn't speak up for himself. One might think that he doesn't communicate well because he doesn't like confrontation.

He has always been taken care of by his older sisters mostly. They always have provided a roof over his head and an excuse for why Patrick couldn't do something for himself. He has always been dishonest with them. Instead of holding him accountable for his actions they have always felt sorry for him and bailed him out. He lived with them most of his childhood and young adult years. Even when he lies, steals and cheats his sisters cover for him.

He has always been the victim. He has been enabled most of his life. His father has always been the victim in his current situation. Neither of them ever seem to take full responsibility for their actions. It is always about what someone else did to cause him to do whatever inappropriate actions taken. Always poor Patrick or poor Patrick's dad. The mother on the other hand, was to blame for all of the family's misfortune because she could not stop being an alcoholic. Since dear old dad was no longer passing out that made him a better more functional drunk.

CHAPTER 36

CHRISTINA AND PATRICK MEET

Let's rewind to January 1991. This is when Patrick met Christina. They met on campus in Florida during undergrad studies. They met in a financial aid line. The lines were so long that all you could do to keep your sanity was talk to other students. They hit it off instantly. They exchanged numbers and dorm information. They would sit and hang out at Christina's dorm all night. Christina would talk Patrick's head off about everything. From her home life to plans to pledge a sorority. He was just so damn nice and such a good listener. Patrick would pay for their food whenever they went out. They mostly hung out at this little chicken shack at the bottom of the hill from campus.

Patrick had friends from Detroit that he went to high school with as roommates. Christina never got too friendly with them. They knew each other. Speaking and a little general conversation was the extent of their relationships.

Christina was pretty sociable. She knew a lot of people. She talked to anyone and everyone. When Patrick expressed an interest in her she told him that she had a boy friend back home in Alabama. The truth was Christina didn't like Patrick that way. She thought he was too nice. She didn't want to hurt his feelings. She just wanted to be friends. Patrick was her best guy friend freshman year.

The following summer they communicated via letters. The next fall they returned to campus. They were hanging even more. They went shopping together. Patrick went to Christina's volleyball games. They went to parties together. Things changed soon after.

Christina pledged a sorority and Patrick got a girlfriend-Nikki. Soon after Patrick dropped out for financial reasons, he and his girlfriend moved back to Detroit. Periodically Christina would ask Patrick's friend Gusto about him. They were out of communication from 1992-1998.

Fast forward to August 1998. Christina was in Detroit visiting a friend from her home town Alabama. They had a cook out and she invited Patrick. They hooked up, talked and reminisced. Christina began to learn more of Patrick's home structure. She felt sorry for him. She thought he was such a nice guy and deserved to be happy.

Soon after they began dating. They began taking trips together. Christina worked for the airline at the time. Patrick was able to travel with her for free. Christina was living in Chicago. By October 1998 Patrick had relocated to Chi-town to be with her. He was waiting on a job transfer. By November 1998 Christina and Patrick decided to get married.

They married January 1999. Two months later Patrick's mother was murdered. Her throat had been cut by a family member for some drug money. Patrick had been living with his parents for who knows how long.

Patrick's dad was put out of the house they were renting. He told Patrick that he needed him to come back home and provide a place for him to live. Patrick discussed this with Christina. She decided to support her husband through this horrible tragedy. She relocated to Patrick's hometown and began their marriage there. Christina feels that was one of the worse decisions she could have ever made.

The most beautiful thing that Patrick and Christina ever did together was their three beautiful children. By September 1999 their first child was born, eighteen months later their second and six years later their third.

CHAPTER 37

THE SIGNS WERE THERE ALL OF THE TIME

When Christina and Patrick were married and living in Detroit, Patrick would always go mia (missing in action). Detroit was Patrick's stomping grounds. Christina was busy being a housewife, stay at home mom and graduate student. Patrick worked full time for a phone company and was in undergraduate school. Therefore, it was pretty easy for him to be away from home without much grief from his wife.

Patrick had this guy friend named Arny. Arny was single. Christina didn't like him much because she felt that he didn't respect their marriage. She felt that Patrick was always up to no good when they were together.

Regardless, he and Patrick were always together. They were together so much that Christina suspected they may be having an affair with each other on the down low. Arny was always the reason Patrick was mia. Patrick would say things like "oh, me and the guys were out at the bar. We left there and went to the park to drink and smoke until 3 a.m." Again, remember, Patrick's mother had been murdered so Christina focused on giving Patrick space to grieve and act out or heal. She focused on keeping her family safe, happy and healthy.

Christina understood that Patrick had some issues but she always believed he loved her and the kids. She believed they were the best thing that ever happened to Patrick. Patrick was respectful and kind when he was with her. However, she did notice that Patrick behaved different when they were alone versus when he was around his family and friends.

When they were alone, Patrick would profess his gratitude for Christina and the children. When they were with family and friends he would act like it was no big deal. When she discussed it with him, he told her that he hadn't noticed and that he would do better. He said that his family was not the touchy feely type and he had never experienced that. Patrick often told Christina that he would not want to live without her or their children. Christina was thankful that she had a husband that was faithful, friendly, kind and loving.

Christina felt Patrick was a good person he just didn't make the best decisions for himself. Christina felt that Patrick was a product of his environment. She felt that he was easily influenced. Patrick would make decisions for him based on what pleased his sisters and father. This was always a source of conflict for the couple. Christina is independent and has always made decisions that were in her best interest regardless of what anyone thinks of them. You could see how this would cause friction. Patrick would try to please Christina and his family at the same time. That simply was not possible. Christina always felt that Patrick's intentions were good. Christina would fuss about Patrick being in the streets too much with the guys. He would smooth it over with her and they would be ok.

Christina was a good wife; she cooked Patrick breakfast before work, made his lunches and made sure that dinner was prepared when he returned home. Patrick got sex whenever he wanted. Patrick got oral sex as well. Patrick didn't want for much, his wife trusted him to a fault. Some may say she was a bit naïve when it came to Patrick. Patrick capitalized on this trust throughout their 9 year marriage.

When Patrick and Christina started dating he told her that he only has 1 or 2 semesters left before he got his undergraduate degree. Seven years later LOL –he got his undergraduate degree. Oops, I guess he wasn't in school taking classes after all. And he hadn't graduated when Christina gave him a graduation party.

Patrick was arrested when they were dating for driving with suspended license. His sister paid the bail for him. He said that he had only one speeding ticket that he had not paid so they issued a warrant for his arrest. Of course, he didn't know this.

Well, after being arrested again once they were married, Christina decided to assist Patrick in taking care of the matter. Obviously, he couldn't be trusted to handle the matter. Christina felt that this affected her as well since he was the primary provider and driving was their livelihood.

After Christina completed her research on the matter, Patrick had 6 unpaid tickets and warrants issued for his arrest in 3 different counties. So, 3 court dates and thousands of dollars later Patrick had his license in good standing again.

The signs were there all the while. At this point Christina has concluded that Patrick has an issue completing tasks. That's no reason to divorce a guy, right? That doesn't make him a bad guy. After all, just look at his fabulous role models-his parents alcoholics, his brothers drug abusers, uncles and friends alcoholics, his dad and uncles womanizers. Does the apple fall far from the tree or what?

Fast forward to 2002. Patrick and Christina relocated to Ohio. Patrick and Christina had a home built from the ground. A new place and new beginnings. They planned to raise their family in Ohio. The plan was whoever started working first the other would stay home with the children and get a job second shift. Christina started teaching in January 2003. Patrick became a stay home dad for the first time.

They were planning to buy and sell real estate. They had two phone lines. One was for personal and the other business. Patrick would give most of his friends the business line. Patrick had an apartment in the basement for his personal manly space. You know the pool table, darts, bath, kitchen and big screen television with surround sound- the whole 9 yards etc. Remember, Patrick has never had anything like this to call his own, neither had anyone in his family.

Patrick and Christina switched responsibilities. Christina worked while Patrick took care of all of the bills and banking. Soon afterwards disconnection notices started coming to the house. Patrick could not hide them fast enough. The first one Christina discovered she began asking questions. Patrick assured her that he had everything handled. He had paid the bills but they had already printed the notices. The mortgage company began sending foreclosure notices. Christina could not believe that Patrick could lie so smoothly about everything. Who lies about taking care of the mortgage and utilities? Wouldn't the lights get turned off when someone does that? He couldn't be lying.

At this time, Christina had managed to have an emergency savings of $6000 from her remaining down payment money and student loans. She asked Patrick to provide her with the emergency savings. The savings had been kept in a safe at their home. Patrick got this bright idea that he was going to put the money in a safe deposit box at the credit union where they banked. His reasoning was so that they wouldn't be tempted to bother it. Now mind you, Christina had been periodically checking with Patrick asking how the transitioning was working out for him. How were the bills? Any monetary emergencies? Patrick would always respond with "things are as smooth as a baby's bottom. Everything is cool sweetheart, I got this covered. You don't have to worry about anything."

Well, we soon find out that this too has been a lie. When Patrick had to provide the emergency savings, all hell broke loose. This was the very first time that Christina saw her husband Patrick as a proven liar. He left the house as if he was going to the bank to get the money and came home an hour later. Only to explain that he didn't have the money. It was all gone. He had spent it on drugs and women. He hadn't paid any bills.

Christina was furious. She went ballistic. She had her sister Rita take the children for a drive. She began to throw stuff. She was cursing. For the first time in their marriage, she called Patrick a liar. They had been married for 5 years at this point. She had never come to the conclusion that Patrick was a no good liar. He had spent all of their emergency savings. The question remained on what? She contemplated ending their marriage after this but smooth Patrick was able to talk his way out of it.

Patrick always plays the victim. He is a master in this role. He has such a sincere, humble and quiet demeanor that people feel sorry for him. Even when he has put himself in the situation. People say things like "oh he's such a nice guy. He didn't mean it. Let's give him another chance." And he never really has consequences for his actions.

After things calm down. Christina asked Patrick for an explanation. Patrick explained that he had tried to handle the bills and they got out of control. He was moving money around and trying to be the man that she thought he could be. He explained that he didn't want to disappoint her by not meeting her expectations. He was spending money on drugs, alcohol and cigarettes.

He said that he was depressed about his mother being murdered and didn't know how to talk to her. He said that he didn't want her to worry. He didn't tell her what was going on with him. Also, he didn't want her to know that he couldn't handle the responsibilities of running the household finances. He felt that she would have no use for him. Whenever there was an issue Patrick would often tell Christina things like he doesn't feel good enough for her. But that would only be after he has been busted in a web of lies.

Being the understanding wife that she attempted to be, she could possibly understand what Patrick was explaining to her. What she couldn't understand were the continuous lies. She told Patrick to trust her enough next time. She explained that they were in this together. She took responsibility for her role explaining that she knew that taken care of the household was her strength.

She hadn't known Patrick to be very independent considering he was living in a raggedy house in the worse area of town with his parents. That was one thing about Christina; she tries to take responsibility for her roles in any given situation. She feels that is how a person learns to grow.

Christina resumed the responsibility of taking care of home again. In resuming her position of taking care of the house she started at the credit union. She and Patrick agreed that they would work things through together. Even though Christina handled everything, she always told Patrick what was going on.

They went to the credit union together. Christina asked the teller about their safety deposits boxes. The teller looked at her as if she was crazy and responded "we don't have safety deposits here." Patrick actually had the nerve to tell her "yes you do."

He tried to get the teller to lie for him. The teller was looking at him like what are you talking about? Christina got angry all over again. Because the nerve of Patrick not only to lie but to get a total stranger to lie for him. What really gives?

This event was a major mile stone in their marriage. She couldn't focus on the bad. She had two children with Patrick and thought that they could work through that situation. She had to focus on how to get their bills and mortgage back under control. Christina is a solution seeker. Patrick had not taken responsibility for his actions. There were no consequences so why wouldn't he continue to be himself? Christina cleaned that mess up and they moved forward.

After all, that was no reason to get a divorce, right? Patrick was a good Mr. fix it around the house. It was great watching him interact with his children. Patrick was thinking "phew. I dodged another bullet. My wife is full of understanding or too damn dumb, either way works for me" Christina had to regain trust in Patrick again. Patrick kept to his strengths-manipulating, conning, lying, cheating and stealing. I mean cutting the grass and taking out the trash until the next dilemma. The signs were always there. Christina didn't take Patrick off of the bank account and that came back to bite her in the ass.

Christina is a very compassionate person. Christina is a outspoken woman. She is honest and trustworthy. What you see is what you get. Therefore, she expects people to deal with her in the same manner. She wears her emotions on her sleeves. She trusts until given a reason not to. Because of these characteristics Patrick has always been able to manipulate any situation.

It was easy for Patrick to divert the attention off of any matter at hand. He has always known that Christina doesn't stay angry long maybe 2 or 3 days maximum. She is a communicator. She wants to understand. He knew if he acts vulnerable and hurt from some of his dysfunctional childhood that she would feel sorry for him and back off. She would want to listen to him. This was her way of being the one that her husband confides in. After all, they were friends in college. They didn't date until 7 or 8 years later. She never wanted to lose the friendship element of their relationship.

The signs were there all the time. One day Christina stayed home from work. The business phone rang. She answered and the woman said "may I speak to Patrick?" she was very polite. Christina said "sure, but who are you and what is your relationship to my husband?" She said that her name was Ivy and she was a bit confused. Christina said why? She said that she didn't know Patrick had a wife. She has been spending time with Patrick considering him for her boyfriend.

Christina said really. So, she called Patrick to the phone. However, she explained to him who was on the phone first. Big mistake. Patrick put the phone to his ear and said no one was there. Christina continued to call that number back. The woman never answered again. Christina lost her cool too soon. She got overly emotional and allowed Patrick too much information.

Obviously, when Patrick said hello the woman gave him an earful and hung up on him. He couldn't concern himself with that though he had his wife to deal with. Patrick swore to God that he wasn't cheating and had no clue who that woman could be. He told Christina that maybe the phone lines got tied up and the lady was trying to reach their neighbor whose name is Patrick from Michigan. He said maybe that was who she was talking about. By that time Patrick had won. Christina didn't talk to the woman long enough to be sure that she was talking about her husband. It was possible for the phone lines to get tied up, right?

Christina was so trusting of Patrick she wondered had his cousins tried to set him up with someone. She had no proof that Patrick was cheating. The nerve of that bastard, he tried to leave the house that night. He said that he was going bowling. He was actually going to fix things or shall we say lie to Ivy. She was bamboozled once more. Needless to say, Christina wasn't quite having that. Patrick has completely got off the hook. Bowling was Patrick's ammunition. He would say he was bowling and Christina wouldn't think twice. She would say have fun. That was how he could go mia (missing in action) in Ohio without being questioned or raising suspicion. A friend advised Christina to drop it and she did.

Christina cut off the business phone and moved forward. She never found out who this woman was. She showed her hand too early in the game. After all it is a game. The fact that not all parties know that they're players in it makes it unbalanced. The signs were always there. By now we should see a pattern. Patrick never faces any consequences nor does he admit doing anything wrong.

There was this one time Patrick and Christina went to eat at Applebee's. The waitress walked up to Patrick and said "Bahamas mama man." Christina says "who is she talking to?" Patrick says "I don't know, that's not me." The waitress then says "that was you." Wouldn't you know that Patrick ordered a Bahamas Mama to drink. He has never ordered a mixed drink since Christina had known him. I guess that was his smooth way of letting the waitress know that it is him but keep it on the hush. Patrick was completely cool and laid back the entire time. The signs were there all the time.

CHAPTER 38

CHRISTINA'S CHARACTER BACKGROUND

She was born in Chicago, Illinois and raised in Birmingham, Alabama. She was raised in a single family home with a strong loving mother, older brother and two younger sisters. Her father was not present much. Her parents divorced when she was 4 years old. She doesn't have many memories from living with her father. She remembers her mother taking care of her and her siblings. Her mom took care of work, home, school, clothes and extra curricula activities. Her mother protected them from danger and harm. She was taught right and wrong, good from bad.

Her mom made rules and when they were broken, there were consequences. She was taught to treat others the way she wants to be treated. She was raised under Christianity principles. She participated in many sports. She wasn't allowed to go to sleep over's. Her extended family included a grand mom, grand uncle, aunts, and cousins.

In high school, she played softball and volleyball. She hung out with upper classmen. She dated mostly athletes. She went to football and basketball games. She went to parties and just hung out with friends. She has never lost a friend due to any kind of betrayal.

Her mother passed away when she was 16. Her mother was her best friend. That was the most traumatic experience of her life. This made Christina stronger. It became a catalyst for how she lives her life, decisions and choices that she makes. She had to become independent very fast. She had to rely on memories of how her mom lived. She needed to set good examples for her sisters. She had two younger sisters to look after.

They were moved from a stable home with rules, safety, peace, happiness, security, and normalcy to the opposite environment.

Grand mom's house was shelter. Grand mom had lost both of her daughters. She took all 8 of the children in to live with her. Not to mention raising her own irresponsible son and his four children. Christina's uncle sold drugs from their house. The cycle began because both his sons began to do the same. There were no rules. People came and went as they pleased. Grand mom was grieving and tired. She provided shelter. Raising children at her age was tough. This is some experience Christina had with negative family cycles.

Christina was blessed enough to have her mom's guidance for 16 years. She was able to emerge out of this environment with self confidence and a five year plan for her life.

Christina lived in this environment for 2 years. She had to make the tough decision of leaving her two younger sisters until she could do better for all of them. After graduating high school, she relocated to live with her great uncle and aunt in Chicago. She lived and worked there until she left for college in Florida. Their home was a refuge. It was a place of stability, support, and love. Her mother had relocated from Alabama after graduating high school. Coincidentally, she too moved in with Uncle Bill and Aunt Ruth. She lived and worked there until she married Christina's father and moved out.

Christina had been offered volleyball scholarships from 5 different colleges in Alabama. However, she felt the need for change. She felt that she couldn't help her sisters until she helped herself. She enrolled in a university in Tallahassee, Florida in January 1991.

She was a very sociable freshman. She met a lot of people. She talked to everyone. She considered two people her best friends' freshman year-Lacheon and Patrick. She advanced academically. She kept in close contact with her younger sisters. She was a good role model for them. She visited and sent for them once per semester. She sent birthday and Christmas gifts. She called weekly. They are all pretty close now. She feels that she lives in a way that her mom could be proud.

She pledged a sorority (crimson&cream) her sophomore year. This gave her the extended family that she desperately needed. Many of her life long friends were made in undergrad. She is the first in her family to graduate from a major university. She learned from older sorority sisters, close friends, reflections and other's life experiences. One thing she learned was that her circumstances were not nearly as bad as the next person. She learned not to pity herself for not having a mom. She learned to be grateful for the time she had with her.

She stopped feeling sorry for herself. She began to learn who she was, what she stands for and gratitude. She began to help others less fortunate than herself. She learned to deal with difficult people without cursing them out. She learned that there are many ways to reach your goals. She became very resourceful.

After graduation from college, Christina relocated to Orlando, Florida. She had another rebirth there. She learned to be more grateful, humble and optimistic. She evolved into a more beautiful and confident woman. She learned to be more appreciative of love ones. She wanted to always make sure that they knew they were loved. Things are not always black and white. Life is colorful. It takes humility, patience, compassion, and understanding for continuous growth.

She learned to always take the positive out of situations and move forward from there. Her life's philosophy is to live her life the way she desires, to take the path not often chosen, and to always follow her heart, as long as her choices don't intentionally harm or hurt anyone else. She is a very happy person with this philosophy. Some may call her unorthodox, loyal, honest, beautiful, loving and simply good people. She feels that she is an extension of her experiences and for that she feels infinitely grateful.

She is grateful for her foundation and experiences. Even the experiences with Patrick. It took her out of her comfort zone. It tested her faith. It allowed her to grow in a way that she hadn't expected.

CHAPTER 39

WISDOM

Change is often resistant but necessary. The decision to divorce was the only solution. Divorce is not the end of the world. It's the beginning of a new way of life. The decision to raise her children without their dad in their everyday life was challenging but necessary. Cycles are real.

Children deserve to grow up in a safe and healthy environment. They are God's gifts to parents. It is our task to do what is safe and best for them until they are independent enough to take care of themselves. We must protect them even if it is from a parent.

Adults have issues that they instill in children both positive and negative. Regardless of our childhood experiences we must do and be better. We must get whatever help we need to heal. It is no longer enough for us guide our children by verbalization. We must lead by good examples.

DSM-IV DEFINITION

Antisocial personality disorder is characterized by a lack of regard for the moral or legal standards in the local culture. There is a marked inability to get along with others or abide by societal rules. Individuals with this disorder are sometimes called psychopaths or sociopaths.

DIAGNOSTIC CRITERIA (DSM-IV)

1. Since the age of fifteen there has been a disregard for and violation of the right's of others, those right's considered normal by the local culture, as indicated by at least three of the following:

    A. Repeated acts that could lead to arrest.

    B. Conning for pleasure or profit, repeated lying, or the use of aliases.

    C. Failure to plan ahead or being impulsive.

    D. Repeated assaults on others.

    E. Reckless when it comes to their or others safety.

    F. Poor work behavior or failure to honor financial obligations.

    G. Rationalizing the pain they inflict on others.

2. At least eighteen years in age.

3. Evidence of a Conduct Disorder, with its onset before the age of fifteen.

4. Symptoms not due to another mental disorder.

ANTISOCIAL PERSONALITY DISORDER OVERVIEW
(Written by Derek Wood, RN, BSN, Ph.D. Candidate)

Antisocial Personality Disorder results in what is commonly known as a Sociopath. The criteria for this disorder require an ongoing disregard for the rights of others, since the age of 15 years. Some examples of this disregard are reckless disregard for the safety of themselves or others, failure to conform to social norms with respect to lawful behaviors, deceitfulness such as repeated lying or deceit for personal profit or pleasure, and lack of remorse for actions that hurt other people in any way. Additionally, they must have evidenced a Conduct Disorder before the age of 15 years, and must be at least 18 years old to receive this diagnosis.

People with this disorder appear to be charming at times, and make relationships, but to them, these are relationships in name only. They are ended whenever necessary or when it suits them, and the relationships are without depth or meaning, including marriages. They seem to have an innate ability to find the weakness in people, and are ready to use these weaknesses to their own ends through deceit, manipulation, or intimidation, and gain pleasure from doing so.

They appear to be incapable of any true emotions, from love to shame to guilt. They are quick to anger, but just as quick to let it go, without holding grudges. No matter what emotion they state they have, it has no bearing on their future actions or attitudes.

They rarely are able to have jobs that last for any length of time, as they become easily bored, instead needing constant change. They live for the moment, forgetting the past, and not planning the future, not thinking ahead what consequences their actions will have. They want immediate rewards and gratification. There currently is no form of psychotherapy that works with those with antisocial personality disorder, as those with this disorder have no desire to change themselves, which is a prerequisite. No medication is available either. The only treatment is the prevention of the disorder in the early stages, when a child first begins to show the symptoms of conduct disorder.

THE PSYCHOPATH NEXT DOOR
(Source: http://chericola57.tripod.com/infinite.html)

Psychopath. We hear the word and images of Bernardo, Manson and Dahmer pop into our heads; no doubt Ted Bundy too. But they're the bottom of the barrel -- most of the two million psychopaths in North America aren't murderers. They're our friends, lovers and co-workers. They're outgoing and persuasive, dazzling you with charm and flattery. Often you aren't even aware they've taken you for a ride -- until it's too late.

Psychopaths exhibit a Jekyll and Hyde personality. "They play a part so they can get what they want," says Dr. Sheila Willson, a Toronto psychologist who has helped victims of psychopaths. The guy who showers a woman with excessive attention is much more capable of getting her to lend him money, and to put up with him when he strays. The new employee who gains her co-workers' trust has more access to their chequebooks. And so on. Psychopaths have no conscience and their only goal is self-gratification. Many of us have been their victims -- at work, through friendships or relationships -- and not one of us can say, "a psychopath could never fool me."

Think you can spot one? Think again. In general, psychopaths aren't the product of broken homes or the casualties of a materialistic society. Rather they come from all walks of life and there is little evidence that their upbringing affects them. Elements of a psychopath's personality first become evident at a very early age, due to biological or genetic factors. Explains Michael Seto, a psychologist at the Centre for Addiction and Mental health in Toronto, by the time that a person hits their late teens, the disorder is almost certainly permanent. Although many clinicians use the terms psychopath and sociopath interchangeably, writes psychopath expert Robert Hare on his book 'Without Conscience', a sociopath's criminal behavior is shaped by social forces and is the result of a dysfunctional environment.

Psychopaths have only a shallow range of emotions and lack guilt, says Hare. They often see themselves as victims, and lack remorse or the ability to empathize with others. "Psychopaths play on the fact that most of us are trusting and forgiving people," adds Seto. The warning signs are always there; it's just difficult to see them because once we trust someone, the friendship becomes a blinder.

Even lovers get taken for a ride by psychopaths. For a psychopath, a romantic relationship is just another opportunity to find a trusting partner who will buy into the lies. It's primarily why a psychopath rarely stays in a relationship for the long term, and often is involved with three or four partners at once, says Wilson. To a psychopath, everything about a relationship is a game. Wilson refers to the movie 'Sliding Doors' to illustrate her point. In the film, the main character comes home early after just having been fired from her job. Only moments ago, her boyfriend has let another woman out the front door. But in a matter of minutes he is the attentive and concerned boyfriend, taking her out to dinner and devoting the entire night to comforting her. All the while he's planning to leave the next day on a trip with the other woman.

The boyfriend displays typical psychopathic characteristics because he falsely displays deep emotion toward the relationship, says Wilson. In reality, he's less concerned with his girlfriend's depression than with making sure she's clueless about the other woman's existence. In the romance department, psychopaths have an ability to gain your affection quickly, disarming you with words, intriguing you with grandiose plans. If they cheat you'll forgive them, and one day when they've gone too far, they'll leave you with a broken heart (and an empty wallet). By then they'll have a new player for their game.

The problem with their game is that we don't often play by their rules. Where we might occasionally tell a white lie, a psychopath's lying is compulsive. Most of us experience some degree of guilt about lying, preventing us from exhibiting such behavior on a regular basis. "Psychopaths don't discriminate who it is they lie to or cheat," says Seto. "There's no distinction between friend, family and sucker."

No one wants to be the sucker, so how do we prevent ourselves from becoming close friends or getting into a relationship with a psychopath? It's really almost impossible, say Seto and Willson.

Unfortunately, laments Seto, one way is to become more suspicious and less trusting of others. Our tendency is to forgive when we catch a loved one in a lie. "Psychopaths play on this fact," he says. "However, I'm certainly not advocating a world where if someone lies once or twice, you never speak to them again." What you can do is look at how often someone lies and how they react when caught. Psychopaths will lie over and over again, and where other people would sincerely apologize, a psychopath may apologize but won't stop.

Psychopaths also tend to switch jobs as frequently as they switch partners, mainly because they don't have the qualities to maintain a job for the long haul. Their performance is generally erratic, with chronic absences, misuse of company resources and failed commitments. Often they aren't even qualified for the job and use fake credentials to get it. Seto talks of a patient who would get marketing jobs based on his image; he was a presentable and charming man who layered his conversations with educational and occupational references. But it became evident that the man hadn't a clue what he was talking about, and was unable to hold down a job.

How do you make sure you don't get fooled when you're hiring someone to baby-sit your child or for any other job? Hire based on reputation and not image, says Willson. Check references thoroughly. Psychopaths tend to give vague and inconsistent replies. Of course the best way to solve this problem would be to cure psychopaths of their 'illness.' But there's no recipe for treating them, say psychiatrists. Today's traditional methods of psychotherapy (psychoanalysis, group and one-on-one therapy) and drug treatments have failed. Therapy is more likely to work when an individual admits there's a problem and wants to change. The common problem with psychopaths, says Sets, "Is they don't see a problem with their behavior."

Psychopaths don't seek therapy willingly, says Seto. Rather, they're pushed into it by a desperate relative or by a court order. To a psychopath, a therapist is just one more person who must be conned, and the psychopath plays the part right until the therapist is convinced of his or her 'rehabilitation.'

Even though we can't treat psychopaths effectively with therapy, it doesn't mean we can't protect ourselves, writes Hare. Wilson agrees, citing the most important factor in keeping psychopaths at bay is to know your vulnerabilities. We need to "realize our own potential and maximize our strengths" so that our insecurities don't overcome us. Because, she says, a psychopath is a chameleon who becomes "an image of what you haven't done for yourself." Over time, she says, "their appearance of perfection will begin to crack," but by that time you will have been emotionally and perhaps financially scathed. There comes a time when you realize there's no point in searching for answers; the only thing is to move on.

THE MALIGNANT PERSONALITY
(Taken in part from MW -- By Caroline Konrad -- September 1999)

These people are mentally ill and extremely dangerous! The following precautions will help to protect you from the destructive acts of which they are capable.

First, to recognize them, keep the following guidelines in mind.

(1) They are habitual liars. They seem incapable of either knowing or telling the truth about anything.

(2) They are egotistical to the point of narcissism. They really believe they are set apart from the rest of humanity by some special grace.

(3) They scapegoat; they are incapable of either having the insight or willingness to accept responsibility for anything they do. Whatever the problem, it is always someone else's fault.

(4) They are remorselessly vindictive when thwarted or exposed.

(5) Genuine religious, moral, or other values play no part in their lives. They have no empathy for others and are capable of violence. Under older psychological terminology, they fall into the category of psychopath or sociopath, but unlike the typical psychopath, their behavior is masked by a superficial social facade.

If you have come into conflict with such a person or persons, do the following immediately!

(1) Notify your friends and relatives of what has happened. Do not be vague. Name names, and specify dates and circumstances. Identify witnesses if possible and provide supporting documentation if any is available.

(2) Inform the police. The police will do nothing with this information except to keep it on file, since they are powerless to act until a crime has been committed. Unfortunately, that often is usually too late for the victim. Nevertheless, place the information in their hands. Obviously, if you are assaulted or threatened before witnesses, you can get a restraining order, but those are palliative at best.

(3) Local law enforcement agencies are usually under pressure if wealthy or politically powerful individuals are involved, so include state and federal agencies as well and tell the locals that you have. In my own experience, one agency that can help in a pinch is the Criminal Investigation Division of the Internal Revenue Service or (in Canada) Victims Services at your local police unit. It is not easy to think of the IRS as a potential friend, but a Swedish study showed that malignant types (the Swedes called them bullies) usually commit some felony or other by the age of twenty. If the family is wealthy, the fact may never come to light, but many felonies involve tax evasion, and in such cases, the IRS is interested indeed. If large amounts of money are involved, the IRS may solve all your problems for you. For obvious reasons the Drug Enforcement Agency may also be an appropriate agency to approach. The FBI is an important agency to contact, because although the FBI does not have jurisdiction over murder or assault, if informed, they do have an active interest in any other law enforcement agencies that do not follow through with an honest investigation and prosecution should a murder occur. Civil rights are involved at that point. No local crooked lawyer, judge, or corrupt police official wants to be within a country mile if that comes to light! It is in such cases that wealthy psychopaths discover just how firm the "friends" they count on to cover up for them really are! Even some of the drug cartel biggies

will scuttle for cover if someone picks up the brick their thugs hide under. Exposure is bad for business.

(4) Make sure that several of your friends have the information in the event something happens to you. That way, an appropriate investigation will follow if you are harmed. Don't tell other people who has the information, because then something bad could happen to them as well. Instruct friends to take such an incident to the newspapers and other media.

If you are dealing with someone who has considerable money, you must realize that they probably won't try to harm you themselves, they will contract with someone to make the hit. The malignant type is a coward and will not expose himself or herself to personal danger if he or she can avoid it.

Update: A thorough article.

I, the creator of this site, am not a psychologist and no special expertise in the subject. I created the site as a public service, because no similar site existed in 2003. I occasionally get sad calls and emails. I urge you to consult either a clinical psychologist or the police depending on the problem you face, and wish you good luck.

PSYCHOPATHY VS. SOCIOPATHY

Hare writes that the difference between sociopathy and psychopathy may "reflect the user's views on the origins and determinates of the disorder."[43]

David T. Lykken proposes psychopathy and sociopathy are two distinct kinds of antisocial personality disorder. He believes psychopaths are born with temperamental differences such as impulsivity, cortical underarousal, and fearlessness that lead them to risk-seeking behavior and an inability to internalize social norms. On the other hand, he claims sociopaths have relatively normal temperaments; their personality disorder being more an effect of negative sociological factors like parental neglect, delinquent peers, poverty, and extremely low or extremely high intelligence. Both personality disorders are the result of an interaction between genetic predispositions and environmental factors, but psychopathy leans towards the hereditary whereas sociopathy tends towards the environmental.[38]

REFERENCES

http://www.mcafee.cc/Bin/sb.html

http://www.wordiq.com/definition/Sociopath

http://en.wikipedia.org/wiki/Psychopathy

CPSIA information can be obtained at www.ICGtesting.com
Printed in the USA
LVOW01s1210180713

343505LV00003B/160/P